Mastering Essential Math Skills

20 minutes a day to success

Book One: Grades 4 and 5

Richard W. Fisher

For access to the
Online Video Tutorials,
go to <u>www.mathessentials.net</u>
and click on Videos.

Math Essentials

ISBN 10: 0-9666211-3-1
ISBN 13: 978-0-9666211-3-6

Library of Congress Control Number: 00136446

Book production by Tabby House
Original cover design: Pearl & Associates
Second edition cover modifications: Juanita Dix

Manufactured in the United States of America

1st printing 2006 (1st Edition)
2nd printing 2008 (2nd Edition)
3rd printing 2010
4th printing 2014

Math Essentials
P.O. Box 1723
Los Gatos, CA 95031
866-444-MATH (6284)
www.mathessentials.net
math.essentials@verizon.net

Notes to the Teacher or Parent

What sets *Mastering Essential Math Skills* apart from other books is its approach. It is not just a math book, but a *system* of teaching math. Each daily lesson contains five key parts: two speed drills, review exercises, teacher tips (Helpful Hints), a section containing new material, and a daily word problem. Teachers have flexibility in introducing new topics, but the book provides them with the necessary structure and guidance. The teacher can rest assured that essential math skills are being systematically learned.

With so many concepts and topics in the math curriculum, some of these essential skills are easily overlooked. This easy-to-follow math program requires only twenty minutes of instruction per day. Each lesson is concise, and self-contained. The daily exercise help students to not only master math skills, but also to maintain and reinforce those skills through consistent review—something that is missing in most math programs. Skills learned in this book apply to all areas of the math curriculum, and consistent review is built into each daily lesson. Teachers and parents will also be pleased to note that the lessons are quite easy to correct.

The book is divided into eight chapters, which cover whole numbers, fractions, decimals, percentages, integers, geometry, charts and graphs, and problem solving.

Mastering Essential Math Skills is based on a system of teaching that was developed by a math instructor over a twenty-year period. This system has produced dramatic results for students. The program quickly motivates students and creates confidence and excitement that leads naturally to success.

Please read the following "How to Use This Book" section and let this program help you to produce dramatic results with your children or math students.

How to Use this Book

Mastering Essential Math Skills is best used on a daily basis. The first lesson should be carefully gone over with the students to introduce them to the program and familiarize them with the format. A typical lesson has been broken down on the following pages into steps to suggest how it can best be taught. It is hoped that the program will help your students to develop an enthusiasm and passion for math that will stay with them throughout their education.

As you go through these lessons every day you will soon begin to see growth in the students' confidence, enthusiasm, and skill level. The students will maintain their mastery through the daily review.

In school, the book is best used during the first part of the math period. The structure and format seem to naturally condition the students to "think nothing but math" from the moment class begins. The students are ready to "jump into the lessons" without any prompting or motivating needed from the teacher. This makes for a very smooth and orderly start each day.

Also, once you have finished the daily lesson, there will still plenty of time to explain related topics, or work on new topics in the basic test or through other sources.

Step 1

Students open their books to the appropriate lesson and begin together. Have students first go to the review exercises, working each problem and showing all their work. If students finish early, they are to check their work in the review section.

Step 2

When you feel that enough time has been spent on the review exercises (usually two to three minutes), call out "Time." The next step is to go to the speed drills. A good signal is to say, "Get ready to add." The students go to the addition drill and wait for the next signal. Then say, "The number to add is '( )'." At this stage the students place the given number inside the addition circle and, as quickly as possible, write all the sums in the appropriate space outside the perimeter of the circle. As students complete the drill, have them drop their pen-

cils and stand or signal in some appropriate way. When enough time has been given, say, "Time." Students then correct the drill as the answers are read aloud by the teacher or a student. The same process is used for the multiplication drill. It is amazing how motivating these speed drills can become in helping students to master their addition and multiplication facts.

Step 3

After the speed drills, work through the review problems with the class. Work the problems on the board or overhead and go through them step-by-step with the students, drawing responses and asking questions as you go. Allow the students to check their own work in this section. This section provides consistent review and reinforcement of topics that the class learns.

Step 4

After going through the review exercises, give a short introduction of the new material. This is where the teacher's unique style and skills come into play. Appropriate concepts, vocabulary, and skills can be introduced on the blackboard or overhead. This should require only a few minutes.

Step 5

After a brief introduction of the new material, go over the "Helpful Hints" section with the class. Be sure to point out that it is often helpful to come back to this section as the students work independently. This section often has examples that are very helpful to the student.

Step 6

After going through the "Helpful Hints" section, go the two sample problems. It is highly important to work through these two problems with the class. The students can model the techniques that are discussed and demonstrated by the teacher. Go through the steps on the board or overhead, and the students can write them directly into their books. Working these sample problems together with the class can prevent a lot of

unnecessary frustration on the part of the students. In essence, in working them together, each student has successfully completed the first two problems of the lesson. This can assist in developing confidence as a routine part of each daily lesson.

Step 7

Next, allow the students to complete the daily exercises and the word problem of the day. Make it a point to circulate and offer individual help. If it is necessary, work another example or two on the board with the entire class. Also, reading the word problem of the day together with the class before they work it independently may be very beneficial.

Step 8

Last, collect the books, correct them and return them the next day. It may sometimes be appropriate to correct them with the students.

Contents

Review Exercises | Speed Drills

1. 342
    + 27

2. 713
    + 24

3. 6 + 7 + 4 =

4. 6
    7
    + 2

1. Line up the numbers on the right side.
2. Add the ones first.
3. Remember to regroup when necessary.
4. "Sum" means to add.

Helpful Hints

S. 453
    + 364

S. 423
    345
    + 223

1. 43
    + 54

2. 67
    + 34

3. 42
    36
    + 25

4. 324
    83
    + 14

5. 426
    314
    + 222

6. 453
    232
    + 632

7. 33 + 24 + 16 =

8. 34 + 216 + 425 =

9. Find the sum of 223 + 15 + 234

10. Find the sum of 16, 17, 12, and 18

1	
2	
3	
4	
5	
6	
7	
8	
9	
10	
Score	

Problem Solving There are 34 boys and girls in Mr. Smith's class, and 38 in Ms. Garcia's class. How many students are there in both classes?

5

Speed Drills

+

7 3 9
0 5
8 1
4 2 6

x

7 3 9
0 5
8 1
4 2 6

Helpful Hints

	1
	2
	3
	4
	5
	6
	7
	8
	9
	10
	Score

Review Exercises

1.　　34
　　　12
　　+ 26

2.　　315
　　　　24
　　+ 234

3.　　42 + 116 + 25 =

4.　　Find the sum of
　　　14, 18, and 24

When writing large numbers, place commas every three numerals, starting from the right side. This makes them easier to read.

Example:　　　5 million, 234 thousand, 216

5,234,216

S.　　2,342
　　+ 3,237

S.　　3,762
　　　 514
　　+ 2,415

1.　　2,437
　　+ 2,564

2.　　　536
　　　　 16
　　+ 3,243

3.　　5,232
　　　1,423
　　+ 2,372

4.　　52,736
　　+　5,521

5.　　7,213
　　　2,314
　　+ 3,516

6.　　2,134
　　　3,213
　　　4,213
　　+ 1,106

7.　　Find the sum of　1,213　and　7,176

8.　　3,512 + 4,213 + 7,232 =

9.　　45,462 + 7,374 =

10.　　Find the sum of 3,712,　4,367,　and 843

6　　One city has a population of 12,213 and another has a population of 8,412. A third city has 13,415 inhabitants. What is the total population of the three cities?

Problem Solving

Review Exercises | Speed Drills

1.   23
     42
   + 43

2.   3,712
     2,314
   + 3,214

3.   Find the sum of 1,234, 372, and 2,314

4.   16 + 172 + 3,752 + 2,713 =

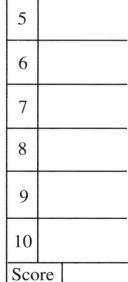

1. Line up the numbers on the right side.
2. Subtract the ones first.
3. Remember to regroup when necessary.
4. It may be necessary to regroup more than once.
5. "Find the difference" means to subtract.
6. "Show how much more" means to subtract.

Examples

$$\begin{array}{r} ^{8}\,^{1} \\ 7\cancel{9}3 \\ -\ 75 \\ \hline 718 \end{array}$$

$$\begin{array}{r} ^{5\ 11}\,^{1} \\ \cancel{6}\cancel{2}3 \\ -254 \\ \hline 369 \end{array}$$

Helpful Hints

S.   435
   - 162

S.   7,352
   - 4,171

1.   337
   - 22

2.   312
   - 71

3.   613
   - 352

4.   712
   - 96

5.   3,124
   - 1,512

6.   7,342
   - 1,435

7.   Find the difference between 134 and 28.

8.   Subtract 336 from 847.

9.   7,833 - 625 =

10.   986 is how much more than 723?

1	
2	
3	
4	
5	
6	
7	
8	
9	
10	
Score	

Problem Solving   76 kids walk to school and 19 take the bus. How many more walk to school than take the bus?

7

Speed Drills	Review Exercises

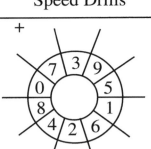

Helpful Hints

1.   48
   + 73

2.   542 - 326 =

3.   372 + 26 + 414 =

4.   742
   - 326

1. Line up the numbers on the right.
2. Subtract the ones first.
3. It may be necessary to regroup more than once.

Examples:

1 9
2 10 13
- 5 6
1 4 7

6 9
7 0 10
- 2 3 4
4 6 6

	1
	2
	3
	4
	5
	6
	7
	8
	9
	10
	Score

S.   502
   - 79

S.   300
   - 167

1.   70
   - 26

2.   300
   - 76

3.   502
   - 65

4.   307
   - 169

5.   6,000
   - 273

6.   760
   - 297

7.   Subtract 376 from 700.

8.   Find the difference between 502 and 96.

9.   7,000 - 269 =

10.   What number is 276 less than 706?

8

Susan earned 276 dollars last week and Phil earned 198 dollars. How much more than Phil did Susan earn?

Problem Solving

Review Exercises	Speed Drills

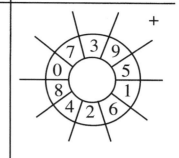

1. 60
  - 27

2. 901
  - 368

3. 303
  - 147

4. 700 - 263 =

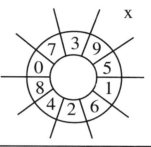

Use what you have learned to solve the following problems.

Helpful
Hints

S. 732
    16
  + 222

S. 303
  - 147

1. 42
    36
  + 17

2. 543
  - 162

3. 7,231
    422
  + 27

4. 761
    243
    143
  + 362

5. 800
  - 126

6. 7,123
  - 281

7. 600 - 208 =

8. Find the sum of 12, 16 and 47.

9. Find the difference between 764 and 149.

10. 23 + 726 + 233 =

1	
2	
3	
4	
5	
6	
7	
8	
9	
10	
Score	

Problem
Solving

A theater has 350 seats. If 243 have been taken by moviegoers,
how many seats are left empty?

9

Speed Drills

+

x

Helpful Hints

Review Exercises

1. 302
    - 68

2. 17 + 23 + 24 =

3. Find the difference between 300 and 182.

4. 5,000 - 347 =

1. Line the numbers up on the right.   Examples:
2. Multiply the ones first.
3. Regroup when necessary. $\overset{1}{2}4$ $\overset{1\;2}{2}36$
4. "Product" means to multiply.   x 3   x 4
                                                          ‾‾‾   ‾‾‾‾‾
                                                          7 2   9 4 4

	1
	2
	3
	4
	5
	6
	7
	8
	9
	10
	Score

S.   35   S.   432   1.   43   2.   25
   x   3   x 6   x   3   x   6
   ‾‾‾‾   ‾‾‾‾   ‾‾‾‾   ‾‾‾‾

3.   232   4.   236   5.   306   6.   3,262
   x   4   x   4   x   3   x   7
   ‾‾‾‾   ‾‾‾‾   ‾‾‾‾   ‾‾‾‾‾‾‾

7.   726 x 4 =

8.   8 x 327 =

9.   Find the product of 184 and 6.

10.   Multiply 7 and 2,133.

10

I have 7 boxes of crayons. Each box should have 32 crayons in it. How many crayons should I have altogether?

Problem Solving

Review Exercises	Speed Drills

1.   23
   x   4

2.   423
   x   6

3.   501
  -   37

4.   37
    426
  + 523

1. Line the numbers up on the right.   Examples:
2. Multiply the ones first.
3. Multiply the tens second.
4. Add the two products.
5. Remember to regroup when necessary.

```
      43           537
    x 32         x  24
    -----        ------
      86          2148
    1290         10740
    -----        ------
    1,376        12,888
```

Helpful Hints

S.   46
  x 23

S.   146
   x   42

1.   16
  x 12

2.   75
  x 16

3.   47
  x 36

4.   124
   x   23

5.   124
   x   30

6.   305
   x   23

7.   Find the product of 16 and 24.

8.   36 x 52 =

9.   Find the product of 52 and 134.

10.   320 x 43 =

1	
2	
3	
4	
5	
6	
7	
8	
9	
10	
Score	

Problem Solving	A small school has only 8 classrooms. There are 32 desks in each classroom. How many kids can go to the school and have a desk?	11

Speed Drills	Review Exercises

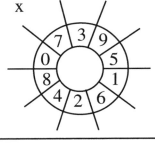

1.   304
    x   6

2.   Find the product of 24 and 36.

3.   724
      35
   + 216

4.   Find the difference between 712 and 96.

Helpful Hints

Use what you have learned to solve the following problems.

S.   423   S.   432   1.   26   2.   304
   x   6   x   23   x   3   x   6

3.   527   4.   47   5.   47   6.   246
   x   6   x   30   x   34   x   23

7.   Find the product of 4 and 216.

8.   30 x 712 =

9.   33 x 219 =

10.   76 x 89 =

	1
	2
	3
	4
	5
	6
	7
	8
	9
	10
	Score

12

Each package of paper contains a ream, or 500 sheets, of paper. How many sheets do 7 reams contain?

Problem Solving

Review Exercises

1.   346
  - 128

2.   312
  x   6

3.   7,653
  + 2,374

4.   Find the product of 23 and 16.

+

x

1. Divide
2. Multiply
3. Subtract
4. Begin again

Examples

$$2\overline{)35} \quad {}^{r\,1}$$
$$1\,7$$
$$-\,2\downarrow$$
$$1\,5$$
$$-\,1\,4$$
$$1$$

$$4\overline{)27} \quad {}^{r\,3}$$
$$6$$
$$-\,2\,4$$
$$3$$

Remember! The remainder must always be smaller than the divisor!

Helpful Hints

S. $2\overline{)37}$ S. $4\overline{)37}$ 1. $3\overline{)43}$ 2. $8\overline{)43}$

3. $7\overline{)87}$ 4. $4\overline{)93}$ 5. $8\overline{)97}$ 6. $6\overline{)43}$

7. $66 \div 5 =$

8. $97 \div 4 =$

9. $\dfrac{61}{5}$

10. $\dfrac{37}{2}$

1	
2	
3	
4	
5	
6	
7	
8	
9	
10	
Score	

Problem Solving A teacher needs 72 rulers for his class. If rulers come in boxes that contain 6 rulers, how many boxes does the teacher need?

13

Speed Drills

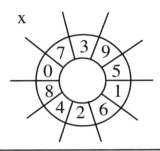

x

Helpful
Hints

	1
	2
	3
	4
	5
	6
	7
	8
	9
	10
Score	

Review Exercises

1. $2\overline{)35}$ 2. $6\overline{)55}$

3.   4 x 236 =   4.   700 - 217 =

1. Divide
2. Multiply
3. Subtract
4. Begin Again

Remember! The
remainder must
always be smaller
than the divisor!

Examples:

$$\begin{array}{r} 1\,7\,1^{\,r\,2} \\ 3\overline{)5\,1\,5} \\ -3\downarrow \\ \hline 2\,1\downarrow \\ -2\,1 \\ \hline 0\,5 \\ -3 \\ \hline 2 \end{array}$$

$$\begin{array}{r} 2\,0\,3 \\ 4\overline{)8\,1\,2} \\ -8\downarrow \\ \hline 0\,1\downarrow \\ -0 \\ \hline 1\,2 \\ -1\,2 \\ \hline 0 \end{array}$$

$$\begin{array}{r} 6\,7^{\,r\,1} \\ 5\overline{)3\,3\,6} \\ -3\,0\downarrow \\ \hline 3\,6 \\ -3\,5 \\ \hline 1 \end{array}$$

S. $3\overline{)\,432}$ S. $3\overline{)\,913}$ 1. $2\overline{)\,512}$

2. $2\overline{)\,819}$ 3. $7\overline{)\,924}$ 4. $5\overline{)\,412}$

5. $6\overline{)\,208}$ 6. $3\overline{)\,614}$ 7. $4\overline{)\,484}$

8. $4\overline{)\,302}$ 9. $8\overline{)\,979}$ 10. $6\overline{)\,953}$

A small theater has 75 seats. The seats are placed in 5
equal rows. How many seats are in each row?

Problem
Solving

Review Exercises	Speed Drills

1. $3\overline{)79}$ 2. $4\overline{)330}$ 3. $\begin{array}{r} 26 \\ \times\ 42 \\ \hline \end{array}$

4. Find the difference between 236 and 84

1. Divide
2. Multiply
3. Subtract
4. Begin Again

Remember! The remainder must always be smaller than the divisor!

Examples:

$$\begin{array}{r} 2\,4\,0\,4^{\ r\,1} \\ 3\overline{)\,7\,2\,1\,3} \\ -\,6\ \downarrow \\ \hline 1\,2\ \downarrow \\ -\,1\,2\ \ \downarrow \\ \hline 0\,1 \\ -\,0 \\ \hline 1\,3 \\ -\,1\,2 \\ \hline 1 \end{array}$$

$$\begin{array}{r} 4\,4\,8^{\ r\,2} \\ 4\overline{)\,1\,7\,9\,4} \\ -\,1\,6\ \downarrow \\ \hline 1\,9\ \downarrow \\ -\,1\,6 \\ \hline 3\,4 \\ -\,3\,2 \\ \hline 2 \end{array}$$

Helpful Hints

S. $3\overline{)\,7062}$ S. $4\overline{)\,3452}$ 1. $4\overline{)\,3452}$

2. $4\overline{)\,6743}$ 3. $4\overline{)\,3426}$ 4. $4\overline{)\,7232}$

5. $5\overline{)\,6555}$ 6. $4\overline{)\,5995}$ 7. $4\overline{)\,1332}$

8. $4\overline{)\,5533}$ 9. $4\overline{)\,1224}$ 10. $4\overline{)3210}$

1	
2	
3	
4	
5	
6	
7	
8	
9	
10	
Score	

Problem Solving Mrs. Toran, has baked 2,112 cookies. If she puts 6 cookies in a box, how many boxes does she need to buy?

15

Speed Drills	Review Exercises

+

x

Helpful Hints

1. Divide
2. Multiply
3. Subtract
4. Begin again

1.　5) 1232　　　2.　　213
　　　　　　　　　　　　　x　　7

3.　　710
　　 - 167

4.　344 + 16 + 245 =

Use what you have learned to solve the following problems.
Remember! Remainders must always be less that the divisor.
Zeroes may sometimes appear in the quotient.

1	
2	
3	
4	
5	
6	
7	
8	
9	
10	
Score	

S.　3) 245　　　S.　8) 8568　　　1.　2)32

2.　5) 750　　　3.　3) 765　　　4.　5) 173

5.　6) 2467　　6.　8) 698　　　7.　6) 1817

8.　3) 7213　　9.　6) 6007　　10.　8) 3209

16

Four boys worked together raking leaves. They earned a total of 224 dollars. If they shared the money equally, how much did each boy get?

Problem Solving

Review Exercises

1. $2\overline{)314}$

2. $703 - 362 =$

3. $\begin{array}{r} 326 \\ \times\ 20 \\ \hline \end{array}$

4. $5\overline{)507}$

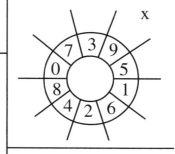

Examples:

1. Divide
2. Multiply
3. Subtract
4. Begin again

$$60\overline{)\begin{array}{l} \overset{1\ \ \text{r }16}{76} \\ -60 \\ \hline 16 \end{array}}$$

$$40\overline{)\begin{array}{l} \overset{4\ \ \text{r }16}{176} \\ -160 \\ \hline 16 \end{array}}$$

$$30\overline{)\begin{array}{l} \overset{1\ 2\ \ \text{r }12}{372} \\ -30\downarrow \\ \hline 72 \\ -60 \\ \hline 12 \end{array}}$$

Helpful
Hints

S. $20\overline{)47}$

S. $30\overline{)672}$

1. $20\overline{)32}$

2. $20\overline{)256}$

3. $50\overline{)635}$

4. $20\overline{)326}$

5. $20\overline{)142}$

6. $50\overline{)655}$

7. $40\overline{)87}$

8. $30\overline{)265}$

9. $50\overline{)608}$

10. $30\overline{)172}$

1	
2	
3	
4	
5	
6	
7	
8	
9	
10	
Score	

Problem Solving A bakery puts chocolate-chip cookies into boxes of 20 each. If 240 cookies were baked, how many boxes would be needed?

17

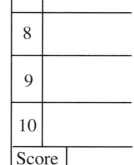

Speed Drills	Review Exercises

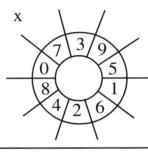

+

x

Helpful Hints

1.   243
        22
   + 216

2.   300
    - 176

3.   242
   x   3

4.   2) 504

Sometimes it is easier to mentally round the divisor to the nearest power of 10.

$$22\overline{)67} \quad \begin{array}{r} 3^{\,r\,1} \\ -66 \\ \hline 1 \end{array}$$

Think of: $20\overline{)67}$

$$31\overline{)97} \quad \begin{array}{r} 3^{\,r\,4} \\ -93 \\ \hline 4 \end{array}$$

Think of: $30\overline{)97}$

1	
2	
3	
4	
5	
6	
7	
8	
9	
10	
Score	

S. $21\overline{)43}$ S. $43\overline{)87}$ 1. $41\overline{)91}$

2. $31\overline{)98}$ 3. $32\overline{)69}$ 4. $23\overline{)69}$

5. $52\overline{)89}$ 6. $42\overline{)89}$ 7. $12\overline{)39}$

8. $31\overline{)94}$ 9. $62\overline{)97}$ 10. $22\overline{)76}$

---

18   A small school has only 150 students. If there are 30 students in each class, how many classes are there?

Problem Solving

Review Exercises	Speed Drills

1. $2\overline{)17}$ 2. $5\overline{)655}$

3. $20\overline{)63}$ 4. $20\overline{)422}$

Remember to mentally round the divisor to the nearest power of 10.

$$22\overline{)463}\quad\begin{array}{r}2\ 1^{\ r\ 1}\\ -44\downarrow\\ \hline 2\ 3\\ -2\ 2\\ \hline 1\end{array}$$

Think of:

$20\overline{)463}$

Helpful Hints

S. $21\overline{)443}$ S. $22\overline{)682}$ 1. $32\overline{)673}$

| 1 | |
| 2 | |

2. $31\overline{)654}$ 3. $42\overline{)888}$ 4. $41\overline{)493}$

3	
4	
5	

5. $23\overline{)687}$ 6. $21\overline{)869}$ 7. $33\overline{)697}$

6	
7	
8	

8. $22\overline{)487}$ 9. $23\overline{)487}$ 10. $32\overline{)999}$

9	
10	
Score	

Problem Solving If a grocer has 13 egg cartons in his cooler, each containing a dozen eggs, how many eggs does he have altogether?

19

Speed Drills	Review Exercises

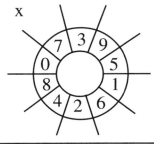

1.　3) 72　　　　　　2.　6) 1332

3.　40) 848　　　　4.　21) 442

Use what you have learned to solve the following problems.

Remember:
Mentally round 2-digit divisors to the nearest power of ten.
Remainders must be less than divisors.

Helpful Hints

| 1 |
| 2 |
| 3 |
| 4 |
| 5 |
| 6 |
| 7 |
| 8 |
| 9 |
| 10 |
| Score |

S.　20) 632　　S.　32) 682　　1.　2) 17

2.　3) 713　　3.　3) 225　　4.　5) 726

5.　3) 5266　　6.　20) 42　　7.　20) 246

8.　30) 269　　9.　22) 468　　10.　31) 687

20　　Mom's SUV gets 8 miles per gallon of gas. If she drives 32 miles while shopping, how many gallons of gas does she use? | **Problem Solving**

1. 23
    + 34

2. 324
      35
    + 232

3. 312 + 223 + 414 =

5. 3,213
    4,414
    + 5,126

4. 3,214 + 515 + 3,126 =

6. 35
    - 14

7. 732
    - 227

8. 900 - 368 =

9. 3,234 - 316 =

10. 6,000 - 367 =

11. 34
     x 2

12. 423
     x 4

13. 3,123
     x 7

14. 26
     x 12

15. 213
     x 24

16. 2) 17

17. 4) 552

18. 5) 1666

19. 30) 642

20. 32) 679

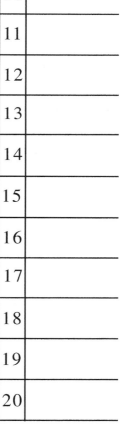

1	
2	
3	
4	
5	
6	
7	
8	
9	
10	
11	
12	
13	
14	
15	
16	
17	
18	
19	
20	

21

Speed Drills	Review Exercises

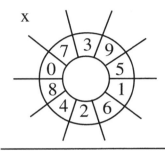

+

x

1.   70
   - 16

2.   23
      24
   + 234

3.   3) 345

4.   224
    x   3

Example:

A fraction is a number that names a part of a whole or a group.

 = $\frac{3}{4}$ → numerator → denominator

Think of $\frac{3}{4}$ as $\frac{3 \text{ of}}{4 \text{ equal parts}}$

Helpful Hints

1	
2	
3	
4	
5	
6	
7	
8	
9	
10	
Score	

Write a fraction for each shaded figure (some may have more than one name).

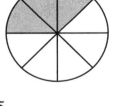

S.   S.   1.   2.

3.   4.   5.   6.

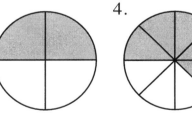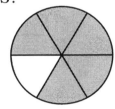

7.   8.   9.   10.

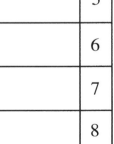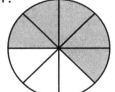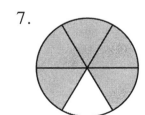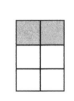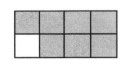

Extra credit: On a separate sheet of paper draw a figure for the following fractions.

$\frac{1}{2} , \frac{1}{4} , \frac{1}{8} , \frac{3}{8} , \frac{2}{3} , \frac{5}{6}$

22   5 boxes weigh a total of 30 pounds. If each box weighs the same, how much does each box weigh?

Problem Solving

Review Exercises

1.   4 x 213 =

2.   16 + 223 + 13 =

3.   510 - 207 =

4.   20) 428

Speed Drills

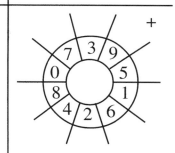

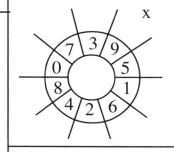

$\frac{2}{4}$ has been reduced to its simplest form, which is $\frac{1}{2}$

Divide the numerator and the denominator by the largest possible number.

$$\bigcirc = \frac{2}{4} = \frac{1}{2}$$

Examples

$$2 \overline{)\frac{6}{8}} = \frac{3}{4}$$

$$5 \overline{)\frac{5}{10}} = \frac{1}{2}$$

$$2 \overline{)\frac{4}{6}} = \frac{2}{3}$$

Helpful Hints

Reduce each fraction to its lowest terms.

S. $\frac{3}{6}$ =

S. $\frac{2}{8}$ =

1. $\frac{2}{10}$ =

2. $\frac{2}{6}$ =

3. $\frac{6}{9}$ =

4. $\frac{10}{15}$ =

5. $\frac{8}{10}$ =

6. $\frac{3}{9}$ =

7. $\frac{5}{15}$ =

8. $\frac{2}{12}$ =

9. $\frac{6}{10}$ =

10. $\frac{7}{14}$ =

1	
2	
3	
4	
5	
6	
7	
8	
9	
10	
Score	

Problem Solving   If there are 12 crayons in each box, how many crayons are there in $1\frac{1}{2}$ boxes?

23

Speed Drills	Review Exercises

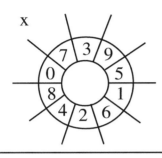

+

x

Helpful Hints

1. What fraction of the figure is shaded?

2. Reduce $\frac{4}{6}$ to its lowest terms.

3. $21\overline{)443}$

4. $\begin{array}{r} 423 \\ \times \quad 20 \\ \hline \end{array}$

An improper fraction has a numerator that is equal to or greater than its denominator. Improper fractions can be written either as whole numbers or as mixed numerals (a whole number and a fraction). To change, divide the numerator by the denominator. Example:

 $= \frac{7}{2} = 3\frac{1}{2}$

$\begin{array}{r} 3\frac{1}{2} \\ 2\overline{)7} \\ -6 \\ \hline 1 \end{array}$

1	
2	
3	
4	
5	
6	
7	
8	
9	
10	
Score	

Change each improper fraction to a mixed number or a whole number.

S. $\frac{3}{2} =$ S. $\frac{9}{6} =$ 1. $\frac{7}{4} =$

2. $\frac{5}{2} =$ 3. $\frac{8}{5} =$ 4. $\frac{10}{7} =$

5. $\frac{6}{4} =$ 6. $\frac{4}{3} =$ 7. $\frac{12}{5} =$

8. $\frac{7}{3} =$ 9. $\frac{11}{5} =$ 10. $\frac{8}{3} =$

24

Saturday 256 people went dancing and on Sunday 168 people went dancing. How many more Saturday dancers were there than Sunday dancers?

Problem Solving

Review Exercises	Speed Drills

1. Change $\frac{6}{5}$ to a mixed numeral.

2. Change $\frac{10}{4}$ to a mixed numeral.

3. Reduce $\frac{4}{6}$ to its lowest terms.

4. What fraction of the figure is shaded?

To add fractions with like denominators, first add the numerators, then ask the following questions about your answer:
1. Is the answer an improper fraction? If it is, convert it to a mixed numeral or whole number.
2. Can the fraction be reduced? If it can be, reduce it to its simplest form.

Examples:

$$\frac{1}{5}$$
$$+\ \frac{2}{5}$$
$$\overline{\frac{3}{5}}$$

$$\frac{1}{8}$$
$$+\ \frac{3}{8}$$
$$\overline{\frac{4}{8}} = \frac{1}{2}$$

$$\frac{3}{4}$$
$$\frac{3}{4}$$
$$+\ \overline{\frac{6}{4}} = 1\frac{2}{4}$$
$$= 1\frac{1}{2}$$

Helpful Hints

S.
$$\frac{4}{5}$$
$$+\ \frac{3}{5}$$

S.
$$\frac{5}{6}$$
$$+\ \frac{3}{6}$$

1.
$$\frac{2}{7}$$
$$+\ \frac{3}{7}$$

2.
$$\frac{4}{7}$$
$$+\ \frac{5}{7}$$

3.
$$\frac{3}{5}$$
$$+\ \frac{3}{5}$$

4.
$$\frac{1}{8}$$
$$+\ \frac{5}{8}$$

5.
$$\frac{5}{6}$$
$$+\ \frac{1}{6}$$

6.
$$\frac{7}{8}$$
$$+\ \frac{2}{8}$$

7.
$$\frac{3}{8}$$
$$+\ \frac{1}{8}$$

8.
$$\frac{7}{10}$$
$$+\ \frac{1}{10}$$

9.
$$\frac{7}{10}$$
$$+\ \frac{5}{10}$$

10.
$$\frac{1}{3}$$
$$+\ \frac{1}{3}$$

1	
2	
3	
4	
5	
6	
7	
8	
9	
10	
Score	

Problem Solving If $\frac{1}{8}$ of the kids in a school ride their bikes to school and $\frac{3}{8}$ walk, what fraction of them either walk or ride their bikes?

25

Speed Drills

+

x

Helpful Hints

1. Add the fractions first.
2. Add the whole numbers next.
3. If there is an improper fraction, change it to a mixed numeral.
4. Add the mixed numeral to the whole number.

*Reduce fractions to lowest terms

Review Exercises

1. $\dfrac{2}{5}$
    $+ \dfrac{1}{5}$
    $\overline{}$

2. $30 \overline{)\,69}$

4. $7 + 14 + 212 =$

3. $\dfrac{7}{10}$
    $+ \dfrac{5}{10}$
    $\overline{}$

Examples:

$3\frac{1}{8}$
$+ 2\frac{3}{8}$
$5\frac{4}{8} = 5\frac{1}{2}$

$2\frac{3}{5}$
$+ 3\frac{4}{5}$
$5\frac{7}{5} = 5 + 1\frac{2}{5} = 6\frac{2}{5}$

$3\frac{5}{8}$
$+ 2\frac{5}{8}$
$5\frac{10}{8} = 5 + 1\frac{2}{8} = 6\frac{2}{8} = 6\frac{1}{4}$

1	
2	
3	
4	
5	
6	
7	
8	
9	
10	
Score	

S. $3\frac{1}{4}$
$+ 2\frac{1}{4}$

S. $3\frac{4}{5}$
$+ 2\frac{2}{5}$

1. $3\frac{1}{5}$
$+ 2\frac{2}{5}$

2. $2\frac{1}{8}$
$+ 3\frac{1}{8}$

3. $2\frac{1}{6}$
$+ 3\frac{2}{6}$

4. $3\frac{1}{10}$
$+ 2\frac{3}{10}$

5. $3\frac{4}{7}$
$+ 2\frac{4}{7}$

6. $3\frac{5}{6}$
$+ 2\frac{2}{6}$

7. $4\frac{3}{8}$
$+ 2\frac{1}{8}$

8. $2\frac{1}{6}$
$+ 3\frac{3}{6}$

9. $2\frac{5}{8}$
$+ 3\frac{7}{8}$

10. $2\frac{3}{4}$
$+ 2\frac{2}{4}$

26

Katie cooks a pie and a cake. She uses $\frac{2}{9}$ cups of flour for the cake and $\frac{1}{9}$ cups for the pie crust. How much flour did she use?

Problem Solving

Review Exercises	Speed Drills

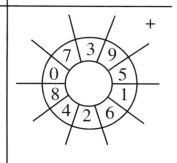

1. Reduce $\frac{6}{8}$ to its lowest terms.

2. Change $\frac{5}{2}$ to a mixed numeral.

3. $\frac{2}{5}$
    $+ \frac{4}{5}$
_____

4. $2\frac{3}{5}$
    $+ 1\frac{3}{5}$
_____

To subtract fractions that have like denominators, first subtract the numerators, then, if necessary, reduce the answer to its lowest terms.

Examples:

$\frac{4}{5}$
$- \frac{1}{5}$
_____
$\frac{3}{5}$

$\frac{5}{6}$
$- \frac{1}{6}$
_____
$\frac{4}{6} = \frac{2}{3}$

Helpful Hints

S. $\frac{3}{8}$
   $- \frac{1}{8}$
_____

S. $\frac{3}{4}$
   $- \frac{1}{4}$
_____

1. $\frac{5}{8}$
   $- \frac{1}{8}$
_____

2. $\frac{3}{6}$
   $- \frac{1}{6}$
_____

3. $\frac{5}{7}$
   $- \frac{2}{7}$
_____

4. $\frac{9}{10}$
   $- \frac{1}{10}$
_____

5. $\frac{7}{11}$
   $- \frac{4}{11}$
_____

6. $\frac{6}{7}$
   $- \frac{1}{7}$
_____

7. $\frac{7}{10}$
   $- \frac{3}{10}$
_____

8. $\frac{7}{8}$
   $- \frac{3}{8}$
_____

9. $\frac{2}{3}$
   $- \frac{1}{3}$
_____

10. $\frac{7}{9}$
   $- \frac{1}{9}$
_____

1	
2	
3	
4	
5	
6	
7	
8	
9	
10	
Score	

Problem Solving   John lives $\frac{4}{5}$ of a mile from school. If he has already walked $\frac{3}{5}$ of a mile, how much farther does he have to go?

27

Speed Drills

+

x

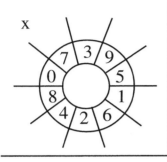

Helpful Hints

To subtract a fraction or a mixed number from a whole number, take one from the whole number and make it a fraction, then subtract.

Review Exercises

1. $\frac{1}{4}$ $+ \frac{1}{4}$

2. $\frac{4}{5}$ $+ \frac{3}{5}$

3. $3\frac{3}{7}$ $+ 2\frac{2}{7}$

4. $3\frac{4}{5}$ $+ 2\frac{2}{5}$

Examples:

$\cancel{3}\frac{}{4} \rightarrow \frac{4}{4}$
$- 2\ \frac{1}{4}$
$\overline{1\ \frac{3}{4}}$

$\cancel{6}\frac{}{7} \rightarrow \frac{5}{5}$
$-\ \frac{3}{5}$
$\overline{6\ \frac{2}{5}}$

1	
2	
3	
4	
5	
6	
7	
8	
9	
10	
Score	

S. 6
$- 2\frac{3}{5}$

S. 7
$-\ \frac{3}{4}$

1. 6
$- 2\frac{4}{7}$

2. 5
$- 1\frac{3}{5}$

3. 7
$-\ \frac{2}{3}$

4. 6
$- 2\frac{9}{10}$

5. 7
$- 2\frac{1}{8}$

6. 9
$- 2\frac{3}{7}$

7. 7
$- 3\frac{7}{9}$

8. 4
$- 3\frac{1}{2}$

9. 6
$- 2\frac{3}{10}$

10. 5
$-\ \frac{3}{5}$

A tailor has 5 yards of cloth. If he uses $2\frac{1}{2}$ yards to make a shirt, how many yards does he have left?

Problem Solving

Review Exercises	Speed Drills

1. $\frac{2}{3}$ $-\frac{1}{3}$

2. $\frac{3}{4}$ $-\frac{1}{4}$

3. $2\frac{1}{4}$ $+3\frac{1}{4}$

4. 196 -128

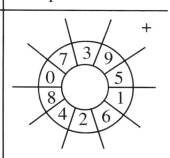

To subtract mixed numbers with like denominators, subtract the fractions first, then the whole numbers. Reduce the fractions in the answer to lowest terms. If the fractions can't be subtracted as they are written, take one from the whole number and increase the fraction, then subtract.

$3\frac{3}{4}$

$-1\frac{1}{4}$

$2\frac{2}{4} = 2\frac{1}{2}$

$\cancel{4}^{3}\frac{1}{4} + \frac{4}{4} = \frac{5}{4}$

$-2\frac{3}{4}$

$1\frac{2}{4} = 1\frac{1}{2}$

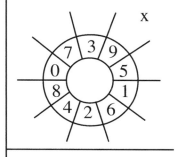

Helpful Hints

S. $3\frac{3}{4}$ $-1\frac{1}{4}$

S. $5\frac{1}{3}$ $-2\frac{2}{3}$

1. $3\frac{3}{5}$ $-1\frac{2}{5}$

2. $4\frac{3}{6}$ $-1\frac{1}{6}$

3. $5\frac{5}{6}$ $-2\frac{1}{6}$

4. $7\frac{7}{10}$ $-2\frac{2}{10}$

5. $3\frac{1}{5}$ $-1\frac{4}{5}$

6. $4\frac{1}{4}$ $-2\frac{3}{4}$

7. $5\frac{1}{7}$ $-2\frac{1}{7}$

8. $3\frac{1}{8}$ $-1\frac{7}{8}$

9. $7\frac{1}{3}$ $-3\frac{2}{3}$

10. $3\frac{4}{5}$ $-2\frac{1}{5}$

1	
2	
3	
4	
5	
6	
7	
8	
9	
10	
Score	

Problem Solving

A woman worked $1\frac{2}{3}$ hours on Monday and $3\frac{2}{3}$ hours on Tuesday. How many hours did she work in all?

29

Speed Drills	Review Exercises

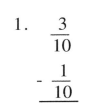

+

x

Helpful
Hints

1. $\frac{3}{10}$
    $-\frac{1}{10}$

2. $\frac{3}{4}$
    $+\frac{1}{4}$

3. Change $\frac{8}{3}$ to a mixed numeral.

4. Reduce $\frac{3}{9}$ to its lowest terms.

Use what you have learned to solve the following problems. Regroup when necessary.

Reduce all answers to lowest terms.

1	
2	
3	
4	
5	
6	
7	
8	
9	
10	
Score	

S. $2\frac{5}{6}$
    $+\quad 3\frac{2}{6}$

S. $5\frac{1}{4}$
    $-\quad 2\frac{3}{4}$

1. $\frac{2}{5}$
    $+\quad \frac{1}{5}$

2. $\frac{5}{8}$
    $+\quad \frac{1}{8}$

3. $\frac{8}{9}$
    $+\quad \frac{2}{9}$

4. $\frac{7}{8}$
    $-\quad \frac{5}{8}$

5. 6
    $-\quad 2\frac{1}{4}$

6. 5
    $-\quad \frac{2}{3}$

7. $3\frac{9}{10}$
    $+\quad 2\frac{3}{10}$

8. $6\frac{1}{3}$
    $-\quad 2\frac{2}{3}$

9. $3\frac{1}{5}$
    $-\quad 2\frac{3}{5}$

10. $4\frac{1}{6}$
    $-\quad 2\frac{4}{6}$

A family has $7\frac{1}{3}$ pounds of beef in the freezer. If they use $3\frac{2}{3}$ pounds for supper, how many pounds do they have left?

Problem
Solving

Review Exercises	Speed Drills

Review Exercises

1.   Find the sum of $\frac{3}{7}$ and $\frac{2}{7}$

2.   Find the difference between $\frac{3}{4}$ and $\frac{1}{4}$

3. 7
     $-\ 2\frac{1}{2}$
     ———

4. $5\frac{2}{3}$
     $-\ 3$
     ———

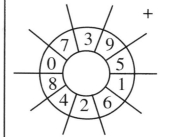

+

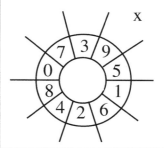

x

To add or subtract fractions with unlike denominators, you need to first find their least common denominator (LCD). The LCD is the smallest number, other than zero, that each denominator will divide into evenly. Examples: The LCD of

$\frac{1}{3}$ and $\frac{1}{2}$ is 6 $\frac{1}{5}$ and $\frac{1}{10}$ is 10 $\frac{1}{4}$ and $\frac{1}{6}$ is 12

Helpful Hints

Find the least common denominators of each of the following:

S. $\frac{1}{3}$ and $\frac{1}{4}$ S. $\frac{5}{6}$ and $\frac{1}{8}$ 1. $\frac{1}{5}$ and $\frac{1}{2}$

2. $\frac{3}{4}$ and $\frac{1}{8}$ 3. $\frac{2}{3}$ and $\frac{1}{9}$ 4. $\frac{1}{5}$ and $\frac{1}{15}$

5. $\frac{4}{5}$ and $\frac{3}{2}$ 6. $\frac{3}{4}$ and $\frac{1}{16}$ 7. $\frac{4}{5}$ and $\frac{1}{4}$

8. $\frac{9}{10}$ and $\frac{1}{2}$ 9. $\frac{3}{14}$ and $\frac{1}{7}$ 10. $\frac{2}{5}$ and $\frac{1}{6}$

1	
2	
3	
4	
5	
6	
7	
8	
9	
10	
Score	

Problem Solving   A plane can travel 700 miles in one hour. If the speed remains the same, how far can it travel in 4 hours?

31

Speed Drills

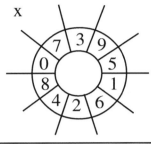

+

x

Helpful Hints

	1
	2
	3
	4
	5
	6
	7
	8
	9
	10
	Score

Review Exercises

1. $3 \overline{)603}$

2. 23×24

3. $36 + 4 + 213 =$

4. $600 - 139 =$

To add or subtract fractions with unlike denominators, find the least common denominator. Multiply each fraction by one to make equivalent fractions. Finally, add or subtract.

*Be sure to reduce all fractions to lowest terms.

Examples:

$\frac{2}{3} \times \frac{2}{2} = \frac{4}{6}$ $\frac{1}{2} \times \frac{4}{4} = \frac{4}{8}$

$-\frac{1}{2} \times \frac{3}{3} = \frac{3}{6}$ $+\frac{7}{8} = \frac{7}{8}$

$\frac{1}{6}$ $\frac{11}{8} = 1\frac{3}{8}$

S. $\frac{1}{4}$ $+\frac{1}{3}$

S. $\frac{4}{5}$ $-\frac{1}{2}$

1. $\frac{2}{3}$ $+\frac{1}{4}$

2. $\frac{2}{3}$ $-\frac{1}{2}$

3. $\frac{4}{5}$ $+\frac{1}{2}$

4. $\frac{2}{3}$ $+\frac{1}{9}$

5. $\frac{1}{2}$ $-\frac{1}{3}$

6. $\frac{3}{5}$ $-\frac{1}{10}$

7. $\frac{2}{5}$ $+\frac{1}{3}$

8. $\frac{1}{4}$ $+\frac{1}{2}$

9. $\frac{7}{10}$ $-\frac{1}{5}$

10. $\frac{2}{3}$ $+\frac{1}{2}$

32   John bought 7 gallons of paint to paint his house. If he used $5\frac{3}{8}$ gallons, how much paint does he have left?

Problem Solving

Review Exercises	Speed Drills

1. $30 \overline{)\ 69}$

2. $\frac{7}{8}$
$-\ \frac{1}{8}$

3. $\frac{1}{4}$
$+\ \frac{1}{3}$

4. $\frac{2}{3}$
$-\ \frac{1}{2}$

When adding mixed numerals with unlike denominators, first add the fractions. If the answer is an improper fraction, first make it into a mixed numeral, then add the sum to the sum of the whole numbers. Always reduce your answer to lowest terms.

Example:

$3\frac{2}{3} \times \frac{2}{2} = \frac{4}{6}$

$+\ 2\frac{1}{2} \times \frac{3}{3} = \frac{3}{6}$

$5 \qquad \frac{7}{6} = 1\frac{1}{6} = 6\frac{1}{6}$

Helpful Hints

S. $2\frac{2}{5}$
$+\ 3\frac{1}{2}$

S. $4\frac{1}{2}$
$+\ 3\frac{3}{5}$

1. $2\frac{1}{2}$
$+\ 3\frac{1}{3}$

2. $2\frac{1}{5}$
$+\ 3\frac{1}{2}$

3. $3\frac{1}{4}$
$+\ 2\frac{2}{5}$

4. $2\frac{3}{4}$
$+\ 1\frac{1}{3}$

5. $2\frac{1}{2}$
$+\ 3\frac{1}{4}$

6. $5\frac{2}{3}$
$+\ 2\frac{1}{6}$

7. $1\frac{1}{2}$
$+\ 2\frac{1}{5}$

8. $3\frac{2}{5}$
$+\ 2\frac{1}{3}$

9. $3\frac{1}{3}$
$+\ 2\frac{2}{5}$

10. $3\frac{1}{5}$
$+\ 2\frac{1}{4}$

1	
2	
3	
4	
5	
6	
7	
8	
9	
10	
Score	

Problem Solving A factory can produce 72 parts per hour. How many parts can be produced in 5 hours?

33

Speed Drills

+

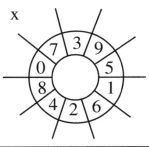

x

Helpful Hints

When subtracting mixed numerals with unlike denominators, first subtract the fractions. If the fractions cannot be subtracted, take one from the whole number and increase the fraction, then subtract. Always reduce your answer to lowest terms.

Review Exercises

1. $\frac{1}{2}$
    $+ \ \frac{3}{7}$

2. $3\frac{3}{8}$
    $+ \ 2\frac{1}{8}$

3. 3
    $- \ 1\frac{1}{4}$

4. $4\frac{1}{3}$
    $- \ 2\frac{2}{3}$

Examples:

$5\frac{1}{2} \ x \ \frac{4}{4} = \frac{4}{8}$
$- \ 2\frac{1}{8} \qquad = \frac{1}{8}$
$\overline{\qquad 3\frac{3}{8}}$

$5\frac{1}{5} \ x \ \frac{2}{2} = \frac{2}{10} + \frac{10}{10} = \frac{12}{10}$
$- \ 2\frac{1}{2} \ x \ \frac{5}{5} = \frac{5}{10}$
$\overline{\qquad 2\frac{7}{10}}$

1	
2	
3	
4	
5	
6	
7	
8	
9	
10	
Score	

S. $3\frac{1}{2}$
    $- \ 1\frac{1}{3}$

S. $4\frac{1}{5}$
    $- \ 2\frac{1}{2}$

1. $3\frac{1}{3}$
    $- \ 1\frac{1}{2}$

2. $4\frac{2}{5}$
    $- \ 1\frac{1}{3}$

3. $3\frac{3}{4}$
    $- \ 1\frac{1}{3}$

4. $5\frac{1}{3}$
    $- \ 1\frac{3}{4}$

5. $3\frac{3}{4}$
    $- \ 1\frac{1}{2}$

6. $3\frac{4}{5}$
    $- \ 1\frac{1}{2}$

7. $4\frac{1}{2}$
    $- \ 1\frac{2}{3}$

8. $7\frac{1}{3}$
    $- \ 1\frac{1}{5}$

9. $3\frac{1}{4}$
    $- \ 1\frac{1}{8}$

10. $7\frac{1}{2}$
     $- \ 4\frac{1}{5}$

34

There are 600 students in a school. If they have been placed in 20 equal-sized classes, how many students are in each class?

Problem Solving

Review Exercises	Speed Drills

1. Reduce $\frac{10}{15}$ to its lowest terms.

2. Change $\frac{12}{5}$ to a mixed numeral.

3. Find the least common denominator for $\frac{1}{2}$ and $\frac{2}{5}$.

4. $\begin{array}{r} \frac{1}{3} \\ + \frac{2}{5} \\ \hline \end{array}$

Use what you have learned to solve the following problems. Remember to reduce all fractions to their lowest terms.

Helpful Hints

S. $\begin{array}{r} 3\frac{1}{2} \\ - 1\frac{1}{4} \\ \hline \end{array}$

S. $\begin{array}{r} 2\frac{1}{2} \\ + 2\frac{3}{4} \\ \hline \end{array}$

1. $\begin{array}{r} \frac{1}{5} \\ + \frac{3}{5} \\ \hline \end{array}$

2. $\begin{array}{r} \frac{2}{3} \\ + \frac{1}{4} \\ \hline \end{array}$

3. $\begin{array}{r} \frac{3}{5} \\ - \frac{1}{2} \\ \hline \end{array}$

4. $\begin{array}{r} 5 \\ - 2\frac{1}{5} \\ \hline \end{array}$

5. $\begin{array}{r} 3\frac{2}{3} \\ + 2\frac{2}{3} \\ \hline \end{array}$

6. $\begin{array}{r} 4\frac{1}{5} \\ - 2\frac{1}{2} \\ \hline \end{array}$

7. $\begin{array}{r} 3\frac{2}{3} \\ + 2\frac{1}{2} \\ \hline \end{array}$

8. $\begin{array}{r} 3\frac{1}{2} \\ - 2 \\ \hline \end{array}$

9. $\begin{array}{r} \frac{3}{8} \\ + \frac{1}{4} \\ \hline \end{array}$

10. $\begin{array}{r} 2\frac{7}{10} \\ + 2\frac{2}{5} \\ \hline \end{array}$

1	
2	
3	
4	
5	
6	
7	
8	
9	
10	
Score	

Problem Solving | Susan earned $3\frac{1}{5}$ dollars on Monday and $5\frac{1}{2}$ dollars on Tuesday. How much more did she earn on Tuesday than on Monday?

35

Speed Drills

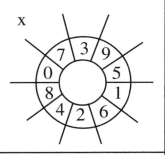

+

x

Helpful Hints

Review Exercises

1. $6 \overline{)726}$

2. $\begin{array}{r} 326 \\ \times\ 4 \\ \hline \end{array}$

3. $26 + 13 + 24 =$

4. $803 - 676 =$

When multiplying common fractions:
- First multiply the numerators.
- Next, multiply the denominators.
- If the answer is an improper fraction, change it to a mixed numeral.
- Be sure to reduce fractions to their lowest terms.
- Remember: "of" means the same as "x" or "times."

Examples

$\frac{2}{3} \times \frac{1}{2} = \frac{2}{6} = \frac{1}{3}$

$\frac{3}{2} \times \frac{3}{4} = \frac{9}{8} = 1\frac{1}{8}$

1	
2	
3	
4	
5	
6	
7	
8	
9	
10	
Score	

S. $\frac{2}{5} \times \frac{3}{5} =$ S. $\frac{4}{3} \times \frac{4}{5} =$ 1. $\frac{1}{2} \times \frac{1}{3} =$

2. $\frac{2}{5} \times \frac{1}{2} =$ 3. $\frac{5}{2} \times \frac{3}{5} =$ 4. $\frac{3}{7} \times \frac{5}{2} =$

5. $\frac{1}{2}$ of $\frac{4}{5} =$ 6. $\frac{2}{7} \times \frac{3}{5} =$ 7. $\frac{3}{2} \times \frac{4}{5} =$

8. $\frac{2}{3}$ of $\frac{4}{5} =$ 9. $\frac{4}{3} \times \frac{5}{6} =$ 10. $\frac{1}{4}$ of $\frac{3}{5} =$

36   Mom cooked a $2\frac{1}{2}$ pound meatloaf for supper, but the family only ate $1\frac{1}{3}$ pounds. How much meatloaf was left for sandwiches?

Problem Solving

Review Exercises	Speed Drills

1. $\dfrac{1}{3}$ of $\dfrac{4}{5}$ =

2. $\dfrac{3}{2}$ x $\dfrac{3}{5}$ =

3. $\dfrac{2}{5}$
   $-\dfrac{2}{5}$

4. $\dfrac{2}{5}$
   $+\dfrac{2}{5}$

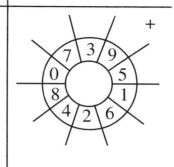

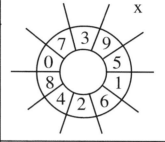

Examples

If the denominator of one fraction and the numerator of another have a common factor, they can be divided out before you multiply the fractions. Remember, "of" means the same as "x" or "times."

4 is a common factor

$\dfrac{3}{\cancel{4}_{1}} \times \dfrac{\cancel{8}^{2}}{11} = \dfrac{6}{11}$

3 and 4 are common factors

$\dfrac{\cancel{9}^{3}}{\cancel{8}_{2}} \times \dfrac{\cancel{4}^{1}}{\cancel{3}_{1}} = \dfrac{3}{2} = 1\dfrac{1}{2}$

Helpful Hints

S. $\dfrac{3}{5}$ x $\dfrac{5}{7}$ =   S. $\dfrac{9}{10}$ x $\dfrac{5}{3}$ =   1. $\dfrac{2}{5}$ of $\dfrac{3}{4}$ =

2. $\dfrac{2}{6}$ x $\dfrac{3}{5}$ =   3. $\dfrac{15}{16}$ x $\dfrac{3}{5}$ =   4. $\dfrac{3}{4}$ x $\dfrac{7}{9}$ =

5. $\dfrac{4}{3}$ x $\dfrac{6}{7}$ =   6. $\dfrac{5}{6}$ x $\dfrac{7}{10}$ =   7. $\dfrac{3}{4}$ x $\dfrac{3}{5}$ =

8. $\dfrac{2}{7}$ of $\dfrac{14}{15}$ =   9. $\dfrac{8}{9}$ x $\dfrac{3}{4}$ =   10. $\dfrac{1}{6}$ x $\dfrac{4}{5}$ =

1	
2	
3	
4	
5	
6	
7	
8	
9	
10	
Score	

Problem Solving There are 15 rows of seats in a theater. If each row has 11 seats, how many people can be seated for a show?

37

Speed Drills	Review Exercises

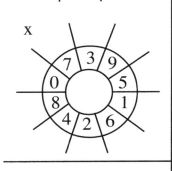

Speed Drills

+

x

Helpful Hints

1. $\frac{2}{3}$ x $\frac{5}{6}$ =   2. $\frac{3}{10}$ of $\frac{5}{6}$ =

3. $\frac{2}{5}$
  $+ \frac{1}{3}$
  _____

4. $\frac{3}{4}$
  $- \frac{1}{3}$
  _____

When multiplying whole numbers and fractions, write the whole number as a fraction, check for common factors, then multiply.

Examples:

$\frac{2}{3}$ x 15 =

$\frac{2}{3}$ x $\frac{\cancel{15}^{5}}{1}$ = $\frac{10}{1}$ = 10

$\frac{3}{4}$ x 5 =

$\frac{3}{4}$ x $\frac{5}{1}$ = $\frac{15}{4}$ = $3\frac{3}{4}$

	1
	2
	3
	4
	5
	6
	7
	8
	9
	10
	Score

S. $\frac{2}{3}$ x 12 =   S. $\frac{2}{3}$ x 5 =   1. $\frac{3}{4}$ x 8 =

2. 10 x $\frac{2}{5}$ =   3. $\frac{4}{5}$ x 20 =   4. $\frac{2}{7}$ x 4 =

5. $\frac{1}{2}$ of 3 =   6. $\frac{2}{3}$ x 9 =   7. 6 x $\frac{7}{12}$ =

8. $\frac{1}{2}$ x 8 =   9. $\frac{4}{5}$ of 10 =   10. $\frac{2}{3}$ x 4 =

38

A class has 32 students. If $\frac{1}{2}$ of the class is made up of girls, how many girls are there?

Problem Solving

Review Exercises	Speed Drills

1.   21) 653   2. $\frac{3}{4}$ x 16 =

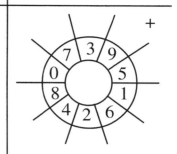

3. $\frac{2}{3}$ x 5=   4. Change $2\frac{1}{2}$ to an improper fraction

To multiply mixed numerals, first change them to improper fractions, then multiply them.

Example:

$1\frac{1}{2}$ x $1\frac{2}{3}$ =

$\frac{1\!\!\!/}{2}$ x $\frac{5}{3\!\!\!/_1}$ = $\frac{5}{2}$ = $2\frac{1}{2}$

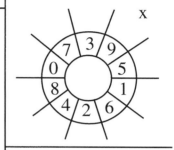

Helpful
Hints

S. $\frac{1}{2}$ x $2\frac{1}{2}$ =	S. $1\frac{1}{4}$ x $1\frac{1}{5}$ =	1. $\frac{1}{3}$ x $1\frac{1}{2}$ =

2. $2\frac{1}{2}$ x 2 =	3. 4 x $1\frac{1}{2}$ =	4. $\frac{2}{3}$ x $1\frac{1}{2}$ =

5. $1\frac{1}{4}$ x $\frac{3}{10}$ =	6. $1\frac{1}{2}$ x $1\frac{1}{3}$ =	7. $\frac{3}{4}$ x $2\frac{2}{3}$ =

8. $\frac{1}{2}$ x $2\frac{3}{7}$ =	9. 2 x $1\frac{1}{3}$ =	10. $1\frac{1}{4}$ x $\frac{3}{5}$ =

1
2
3
4
5
6
7
8
9
10
Score

Problem Solving: A man being chased by a dog can run 6 miles per hour. How far can he run in $1\frac{1}{2}$ hours?

39

Speed Drills | Review Exercises

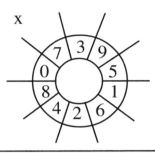

+

x

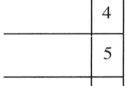

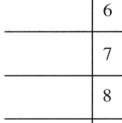

Helpful Hints

Review Exercises

1. $\dfrac{1}{5}$
    $+\dfrac{1}{6}$
    _____

2. $\dfrac{3}{5}$
    $-\dfrac{1}{2}$
    _____

3. $\dfrac{2}{3}$ x $\dfrac{6}{7}$ =

4. $\dfrac{1}{4}$ x 8 =

To find the reciprocal of a common fraction, invert the fraction.

To find the reciprocal of a mixed numeral, first change the mixed number to an improper fraction, then invert it.

To find the reciprocal of a whole number, first make a fraction, then invert it.

Examples

The reciprocal of:

$\dfrac{3}{5}$ is $\dfrac{5}{3}$ or $1\dfrac{2}{3}$

$2\dfrac{1}{2} = \dfrac{5}{2}$ is $\dfrac{2}{5}$

$7 = \dfrac{7}{1}$ is $\dfrac{1}{7}$

1	
2	
3	
4	
5	
6	
7	
8	
9	
10	
	Score

Find the reciprocals of each number:

S. $\dfrac{3}{4}$ S. $1\dfrac{1}{2}$ 1. $\dfrac{1}{3}$

2. $\dfrac{7}{8}$ 3. $1\dfrac{1}{3}$ 4. 12

5. $\dfrac{2}{5}$ 6. $\dfrac{1}{7}$ 7. 5

8. $\dfrac{2}{3}$ 9. $\dfrac{1}{8}$ 10. $3\dfrac{1}{2}$

40   Four boys decided to wash cars to earn money. They washed 12 cars and earned 84 dollars. If they divided it equally, how much did each boy get? | **Problem Solving**

Review Exercises	Speed Drills

1.   Find the reciprocal of 5.

2.   Find the reciprocal of $\frac{2}{3}$.

3.   Find the reciprocal of $1\frac{1}{4}$.   4. $\frac{1}{2} \times \frac{2}{3} =$

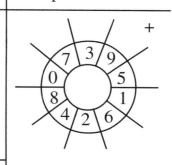

To divide fractions, first find the reciprocal of the second number, then multiply the fractions.

Examples:

$\frac{2}{3} \div \frac{1}{2} =$ $1\frac{1}{2} \div 2 =$ $2\frac{1}{2} \div 1\frac{1}{2} =$

$\frac{2}{3} \times \frac{2}{1} = \frac{4}{3} = 1\frac{1}{3}$ $\frac{3}{2} \times \frac{1}{2} = \frac{3}{4}$ $\frac{5}{2} \div \frac{3}{2} =$

$\frac{5}{\cancel{2}} \times \frac{\cancel{2}}{3} = 1\frac{2}{3}$

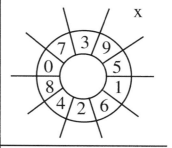

Helpful Hints

1	
2	
3	
4	
5	
6	
7	
8	
9	
10	
Score	

S. $\frac{1}{2} \div \frac{1}{3} =$ S. $2\frac{1}{2} \div 2 =$ 1. $\frac{2}{3} \div \frac{1}{2} =$

2. $\frac{3}{5} \div \frac{1}{3} =$ 3. $\frac{2}{5} \div \frac{1}{2} =$ 4. $\frac{2}{5} \div 3 =$

5. $3 \div \frac{1}{2} =$ 6. $1\frac{1}{2} \div \frac{1}{2} =$ 7. $2\frac{1}{2} \div \frac{1}{2} =$

8. $2\frac{1}{6} \div 2 =$ 9. $\frac{2}{7} \div \frac{1}{3} =$ 10. $5 \div \frac{5}{6} =$

Problem Solving   The coach wants a field which is 36 yards long divided into 3 equal sections for a relay race course. How long will each section be?

41

Reviewing All Fraction Operations

	1
	2
	3
	4
	5
	6
	7
	8
	9
	10
	11
	12
	13
	14
	15
	16
	17
	18
	19
	20

1. $\dfrac{2}{5}$
$+\ \dfrac{1}{5}$

2. $\dfrac{7}{8}$
$+\ \dfrac{2}{8}$

3. $\dfrac{2}{5}$
$+\ \dfrac{1}{2}$

4. $3\dfrac{2}{5}$
$+\ 2\dfrac{4}{5}$

5. $2\dfrac{1}{2}$
$+\ 3\dfrac{1}{3}$

6. $2\dfrac{3}{5}$
$+\ 2\dfrac{1}{2}$

7. $\dfrac{5}{8}$
$-\ \dfrac{1}{8}$

8. 7
$-\ 2\dfrac{1}{4}$

9. $3\dfrac{1}{2}$
$-\ 1\dfrac{1}{3}$

10. $5\dfrac{1}{5}$
$-\ 2\dfrac{1}{2}$

11. $\dfrac{1}{3} \times \dfrac{2}{5} =$

12. $\dfrac{3}{4} \times \dfrac{5}{6} =$

13. $\dfrac{3}{4} \times 8 =$

14. $\dfrac{1}{2} \times 2\dfrac{1}{2} =$

15. $1\dfrac{1}{3} \times 1\dfrac{1}{4} =$

16. $\dfrac{1}{3} \div \dfrac{1}{2} =$

17. $\dfrac{1}{3} \div \dfrac{2}{5} =$

18. $3 \div \dfrac{1}{2} =$

19. $2\dfrac{1}{2} \div 2 =$

20. $1\dfrac{1}{3} \div 1\dfrac{1}{2} =$

42

Review Exercises	Speed Drills

1.   23
      16
    + 12

2. $\frac{2}{3}$
    − $\frac{1}{2}$

3. $\frac{3}{4}$
    + $\frac{1}{3}$

4.   2 , 7 6 3
    −   4 3 7

To read decimals, first read the whole number. Next, read the decimal point as "and." Then read the number after the decimal point and its place value.

ones
tens
hundreths
thousandths
ten thousandths
hundred thousandths
millionths

1 . 2   3   4   5   6   7

Examples:

3 . 2 = Three and two tenths

. 0 0 7 = Seven thousandths

1 4 . 1 6 = Fourteen and sixteen hundredths

Helpful
Hints

Express each of the following numbers as words. Write your answer on the line below the number.

S.   2 . 6

S.   12 . 07

1.   . 6

2.   1 . 7

3.   4 . 0 0 7

4.   5 . 1 6

5.   1 7 . 0 1 2

6.   . 1 3

7.   4 . 4 2

8.   6 . 0 3

9.   6 . 0 0 3

10.   . 0 9

| Score |

| Problem Solving | Maria has 35 trading cards. Susan has three time as many as Maria has. How many cards does Susan have? | 43 |

Speed Drills	Review Exercises

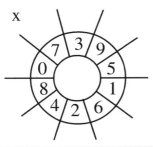

+

x

Helpful Hints

1. 24
   x 23

2. $\frac{2}{3}$ x $\frac{1}{4}$ =

3. $1\frac{1}{2} \div \frac{1}{2}$ =

4. $2 \div \frac{2}{3}$ =

When reading decimals, remember "and" means decimal point. The fraction part of the decimal ends in "th" or "ths." Be careful about placeholders. Examples:

Four and eight tenths = 4 . 8

Two and seventeen hundredths = 2 . 1 7

Nine thousandths = . 0 0 9

1	
2	
3	
4	
5	
6	
7	
8	
9	
10	
Score	

Write each of the following numbers as decimals. Use the diagram at the bottom of the page if you need help.

S.   Two and six tenths
S.   Three and twelve hundredths
1.   Nine and eight tenths
2.   Two and seventeen hundredths
3.   Thirty-two hundredths
4.   Twenty-two and five tenths
5.   Six thousandths
6.   Two and seven thousandths
7.   Eight and two tenths
8.   Eight and two hundredths
9.   Two and seventeen thousandths
10. Twenty-five hundredths

ones tenths hundredths thousandths ten thousandths hundred thousandths millionths

1 . 2 3 4 5 6 7

44   If "normal" temperature for a human is 98 $\frac{3°}{5}$ and a man has a temperature of 98 $\frac{4°}{5}$. How much above normal is his temperature?

Problem Solving

Review Exercises	Speed Drills

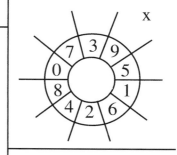

1. $\dfrac{1}{4} \div \dfrac{1}{3} =$ **2.** $1\dfrac{1}{2} \div \dfrac{1}{2} =$

3. $\dfrac{3}{4} \div 2 =$ **4.** $\dfrac{2}{3} \div 1\dfrac{1}{2} =$

When changing mixed numerals to decimals, remember to place a decimal after the whole number.

Examples: $3\dfrac{3}{10} = 3.3$ $3\dfrac{9}{100} = 3.09$

$\dfrac{16}{100} = .16$ $\dfrac{7}{1,000} = .007$

Helpful Hints

Write each of the following as a decimal. Use the chart at the bottom of the page if you need help.

S. $7\dfrac{7}{10}$ **S.** $9\dfrac{7}{100}$ **1.** $12\dfrac{32}{100}$ **2.** $\dfrac{7}{100}$

3. $72\dfrac{9}{10}$ **4.** $72\dfrac{9}{100}$ **5.** $\dfrac{16}{1,000}$ **6.** $7\dfrac{18}{100}$

7. $6\dfrac{12}{1,000}$ **8.** $4\dfrac{6}{100}$ **9.** $12\dfrac{6}{10}$ **10.** $7\dfrac{19}{1,000}$

ones   tenths   hundredths   thousandths   ten thousandths   hundred thousandths   millionths

1 . 2 3 4 5 6 7

1	
2	
3	
4	
5	
6	
7	
8	
9	
10	
Score	

Problem Solving   One block is $\dfrac{1}{2}$ inch high. How high would a stack of 6 blocks be?

45

Speed Drills	Review Exercises

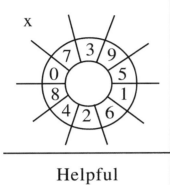

Speed Drills

+

x

Helpful
Hints

1. $\frac{1}{5}$
   $+ \frac{2}{5}$

2. 5
   $- 2\frac{1}{7}$

3. $\frac{4}{5} \times \frac{3}{8} =$

4. $1\frac{1}{2} \div \frac{1}{4} =$

Decimals can easily be changed to mixed numerals and fractions. Remember that the whole number is always to the left of the decimal point.

Examples:

$2.6 = 2\frac{6}{10}$ $.21 = \frac{21}{100}$

$3.07 = 3\frac{7}{100}$ $1.012 = 1\frac{12}{1,000}$

Change each of the following to a mixed numeral or a fraction. Use the chart if you need help.

S. $3.2 =$ S. $5.003 =$ 1. $5.6 =$

2. $.07 =$ 3. $6.09 =$ 4. $7.9 =$

5. $13.015 =$ 6. $.019 =$ 7. $7.008 =$

8. $9.07 =$ 9. $.008 =$ 10. $5.725 =$

1	
2	
3	
4	
5	
6	
7	
8	
9	
10	
Score	

ones tenths hundredths thousandths ten thousandths hundred thousandths millionths

1 . 2 3 4 5 6 7

46

A classroom has 5 rows of chairs, each with 6 chairs in it. Three of the chairs are empty. How many chairs are taken?

Problem
Solving

Review Exercises	Speed Drills

1. Reduce $\frac{6}{10}$ to its lowest terms.

2. Change $\frac{7}{2}$ to a mixed numral.

3. Write 2.7 in words.

4. Change 3.08 to a mixed numeral.

Zeroes can be put to the right of a decimal without changing its value. This helps when comparing values of decimals.

< means "less than."
> means "greater than."
Examples:

Compare 2.3 and 2.7

    2.3 < 2.7

Compare 4.3 and 4.28

4.3 = 4.30 so 4.3 > 4.28

Helpful Hints

Place a < or a > to compare each pair of decimals.

S.   7.6 ☐ 7.3   S.   .2 ☐ .17   1.   6.7 ☐ 5.9

2.   8.3 ☐ 8.9   3.   .4 ☐ .51   4.   .4 ☐ .51

5.   .12 ☐ .3   6.   .7 ☐ .72   7.   3.8 ☐ 3.21

8.   .3 ☐ .005   9.   2.31 ☐ 2.49   10.   6.2 ☐ 6.13

1	
2	
3	
4	
5	
6	
7	
8	
9	
10	
Score	

Problem Solving A scout troop is planning a 28-mile hike. If they hike 7 miles per day, how many days will the hike take?

47

Speed Drills	Review Exercises

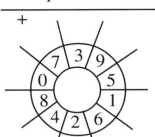

1. $\dfrac{2}{5} \div \dfrac{1}{2} =$ 2. $\dfrac{2}{5} \div 2 =$

3. $\dfrac{3}{8}$ 4. $2\dfrac{3}{5}$
    $+ \dfrac{1}{8}$ $+ 3\dfrac{3}{5}$

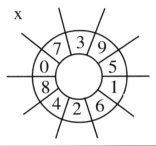

To add decimals, first line up the decimal points vertically, then add as you do whole numbers. Be sure you put the decimal point in your answer. Sometimes you need to put zeroes to the right of the decimal point as place holders.

Example:

$3.16 + 2.4 + 6 =$

$$\begin{array}{r} 3.16 \\ 2.40 \\ +\ 6.00 \\ \hline 11.56 \end{array}$$

Helpful Hints

1	
2	
3	
4	
5	
6	
7	
8	
9	
10	
Score	

S. $\begin{array}{r} 3.16 \\ 2.3 \\ +\ 3.26 \end{array}$ S. $2.24 + 3.4 + .23 =$ 1. $3.14 + 1.4 + 2.17 =$

2. $5.22 + 3.13 + .3 =$ 3. $\begin{array}{r} 4.263 \\ +\ 3.23 \end{array}$ 4. $.34 + .6 + .27 =$

5. $\begin{array}{r} 9.63 \\ 2. \\ +\ 3.7 \end{array}$ 6. $.24 + 3.6 + 7.2 =$ 7. $\begin{array}{r} .3 \\ .4 \\ +\ .4 \end{array}$

8. $\begin{array}{r} 3.63 \\ +\ 4.64 \end{array}$ 9. $\begin{array}{r} 7.12 \\ .136 \\ +\ 2.14 \end{array}$ 10. $3.24 + 2.6 + 3.15 =$

48   In March it rained 3.6 inches and in April there was 2.7 inches of rain. What was the total amount of rainfall for the two months? | Problem Solving

Review Exercises	Speed Drills

1.   3.4
        2.16
   + 3.22

2.   3.6 + 2 + 2.3 =

3. $\dfrac{1}{3}$
     $\dfrac{9}{10}$
 +

4.   Write $3\dfrac{7}{100}$ as a decimal.

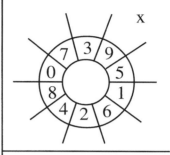

To subtract decimals, first line up the decimal points vertically, then subtract as you do whole numbers. Be sure you put the decimal point in your answer. Sometimes you need to put zeroes to the right of the decimal point as place holders.

  Examples:

$3.2 - 1.62 =$
$$\overset{2}{\cancel{3}}.\overset{11}{\cancel{2}}{}_10$$
$$-\ 1.62$$
$$1.58$$

$7 - 1.63 =$
$$\overset{6}{\cancel{7}}.\overset{9}{\cancel{0}}{}_10$$
$$-\ 1.63$$
$$5.37$$

Helpful
Hints

S.   7.21
   - 3.13

S.   6.8 - 3.14 =

1.   6.2
   - 3.17

2.   3.26
   - 1.34

3.   5.1
   - 2.43

4.   13.6 - 8.8 =

5.   .7
   - .62

6.   7.43
   - 2.16

7.   3 - 1.6 =

8.   .23
   - .124

9.   13.2 - 7.16 =

10.   7.32
    - 4.25

1	
2	
3	
4	
5	
6	
7	
8	
9	
10	
Score	

Problem Solving   Bill ran a race in 9.6 seconds. Jane ran the race in 8.4 seconds. How much longer did it take Bill to run the race than Jane?

49

Speed Drills	Review Exercises

+

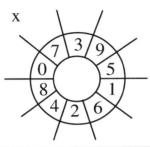

x

Helpful
Hints

1. $\frac{1}{3}$
    $-\frac{1}{3}$

2. $\frac{3}{8}$
    $+\frac{3}{8}$

3. $\frac{4}{5}$
    $+\frac{4}{5}$

4. $\frac{1}{3}$
    $+\frac{2}{3}$
    $\frac{1}{3}$

Use what you have learned to
solve the following problems.

Remember:
Line up the decimals.
Put the decimal in your answer.
Zeroes may be added to the right of the decimal point.

1	
2	
3	
4	
5	
6	
7	
8	
9	
10	
Score	

S.   2.3
     3.14
   + .32

S.   7.6
   - 2.34

1.   2.45
   + 3.23

2.   3.2
   - 1.4

3.   3.24
     2.42
   + 3.43

4.   6.2
   - 3.16

5.   7 - 2.6 =

6.   .7
     .2
   + .4

7.   7.61
   - 2.43

8.   5.21 + 2.6 + 3.23 =

9.   5 – 1.2 =

10. 7.3
     2.43
   + 3.24

50

A boy earned $7.95 washing his uncle's car. If he spends $3.34
on his way home, how much does he have left?

Problem
Solving

Review Exercises	Speed Drills

1.   24   2.   232   3.   24   4.   124
   x   3   x   4   x 23   x 23

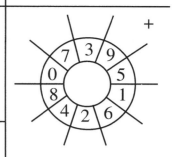

Multiply as you would with whole numbers. Count the number of decimal places and place the decimal point properly in the product.

Examples:

2.32 ← 2 places
x   3
6.96 ← 2 places

1.4 ← 1 place
x 2 3
4 2
2 8 0
3 2 .2 ← 1 place

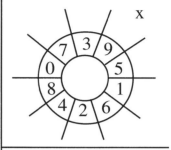

Helpful
Hints

S. 3.43	S. 4.3	1. 2.15	1
x 2	x 1.2	x 3	2
2. .423	3. 53.2	4. 2.4	3
x 2	x 4	x 2 3	4
5. 2.32	6. 2.6	7. 5.14	5
x 23	x 2 2	x 3	6
8. 43.2	9. .234	10. 3.6	7
x 6	x 4	x 3 2	8
			9
			10
			Score

Problem Solving	An old man is only able to walk 2.4 miles in an hour. If he walks for three hours, how far will he go?	51

Speed Drills	Review Exercises

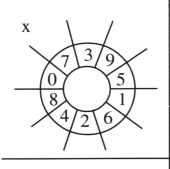

x

Helpful Hints

1.   2.3
    x   3

2.   4.2
    x   1 2

3. $\dfrac{2}{5}$ x $\dfrac{1}{4}$ =

4. $\dfrac{1}{2}$ ÷ $\dfrac{1}{3}$ =

Multiply as you would with whole numbers. Find the total number of decimal places in all numerals, and place the decimal point properly in the product.

Examples:

$$4.3 \leftarrow \text{1 place}$$
$$\underline{x \quad 2.1} \leftarrow \text{1 place}$$
$$4\,3$$
$$\underline{8\,6\,0}$$
$$9.0\,3 \leftarrow \text{2 places}$$

$$2.43 \leftarrow \text{2 places}$$
$$\underline{x \; .2} \leftarrow \text{1 place}$$
$$.486 \leftarrow \text{3 places}$$

1	
2	
3	
4	
5	
6	
7	
8	
9	
10	
	Score

S.   3.2
   x   .2

S.   4.12
   x   2.3

1.   .42
   x   .3

2.   6.3
   x   .2

3.   21.4
   x   .3

4.   2.4
   x   1.3

5.   4.1
   x .3 2

6.   3.42
   x   4.3

7.   2.13
   x   .5

8.   1.24
   x   .6

9.   4.2
   x   3.4

10.   12.4
   x   .3

A woman does laundry six days a week to support her children. She earns 16 dollars each day. How much does she earn in a week?

Problem Solving

Review Exercises	Speed Drills

1. $2\frac{1}{2} \div \frac{1}{2} =$ 2. $2 \times 1\frac{1}{2} =$

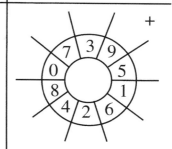

3. $\frac{4}{9} \times \frac{3}{8} =$ 4. $5 \div \frac{1}{2} =$

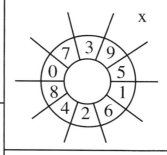

Use what you have learned to solve the following problems.

* Be careful when placing the decimal in the product.

Helpful
Hints

S.   2 . 4   S.   4 . 2   1.   1 . 2 3
      x   3   x . 5   x   3

2.   3 4 . 3   3.   . 1 4   4.   . 3 4
      x   . 4   x 2 3   x   2.4

5.   3 1 . 2   6.   2 . 4 3   7.   . 4 3 6
      x   6   x   1.2   x   2

8.   4 . 3 2   9.   2 . 4 3   10.   2.5
      x   . 4   x   . 5   x   2 3

1	
2	
3	
4	
5	
6	
7	
8	
9	
10	
Score	

Problem Solving | A store has shirts on sale for $7.24 each. How much money would John need to buy 3 shirts?

53

Speed Drills	Review Exercises

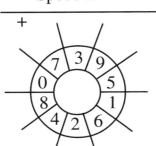

1. $2\overline{)42}$ 2. $3\overline{)13.2}$

3. $3\overline{)7261}$ 4. $20\overline{)469}$

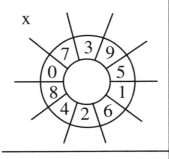

Helpful Hints

Divide just as you do with whole numbers. Place the decimal points directly up.

Be careful. Sometimes place holders are necessary

Examples:

$$\begin{array}{r} 2.3 \\ 3\overline{)6.9} \\ -6\downarrow \\ \hline 9 \\ -9 \\ \hline 0 \end{array}$$

$$\begin{array}{r} .045 \\ 3\overline{).135} \\ -12\downarrow \\ \hline 15 \\ -15 \\ \hline 0 \end{array}$$

	1
	2
	3
	4
	5
	6
	7
	8
	9
	10
	Score

S. $2\overline{)4.6}$ S. $3\overline{)13.2}$ 1. $2\overline{)2.6}$

2. $2\overline{)1.72}$ 3. $4\overline{)53.2}$ 4. $3\overline{)1.53}$

5. $5\overline{)21.35}$ 6. $3\overline{)6.45}$ 7. $4\overline{).928}$

8. $5\overline{)1.725}$ 9. $3\overline{)6.69}$ 10. $2\overline{)13.2}$

A man buys four 12-foot boards. He wants to make shelves that are 3-feet long. How many shelves can he make from his boards?

Problem Solving

Review Exercises	Speed Drills

1. $3\overline{)6.54}$ 2. $5\overline{)1.5}$

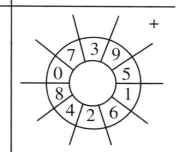

3. $2.42 + 3 + 1.2 =$ 4. 5.2
                                               -3.6

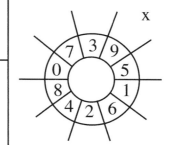

Sometimes place holders are necessary when dividing decimals.

Examples:

$$3\overline{)\begin{array}{r} .05 \\ .15 \\ -15 \\ \hline 0 \end{array}}$$

$$4\overline{)\begin{array}{r} .0004 \\ .0016 \\ -16 \\ \hline 0 \end{array}}$$

Helpful Hints

S. $2\overline{).014}$ S. $3\overline{).132}$ 1. $7\overline{).049}$

2. $2\overline{).114}$ 3. $4\overline{).224}$ 4. $5\overline{).015}$

5. $9\overline{).027}$ 6. $4\overline{).056}$ 7. $2\overline{).012}$

8. $3\overline{).102}$ 9. $4\overline{).324}$ 10. $6\overline{).246}$

1	
2	
3	
4	
5	
6	
7	
8	
9	
10	
Score	

Problem Solving Alex earned $7.25 on Monday and $5.40 on Tuesday. How much more did he earn on Monday than on Tuesday?

55

Speed Drills	Review Exercises

+

x

1.   3.23
      1.2
   + .36

2.   7.23
   - 2.15

3.   3.12
   x 7

4.   2) 3.2

Sometimes zeroes need to be added to the dividend to complete the problem.

Examples:

$$5 \overline{)\ 1.3} = 5 \overline{)\ 1.30}$$
$$\begin{array}{r} .26 \\ \underline{-10\downarrow} \\ 30 \\ \underline{-30} \\ 0 \end{array}$$

$$2 \overline{)\ .2\ 3} = 2 \overline{)\ .2\ 3\ 0}$$
$$\begin{array}{r} .1\ 1\ 5 \\ \underline{-2\downarrow} \\ 0\ 3\downarrow \\ \underline{-2} \\ 1\ 0 \\ \underline{-1\ 0} \\ 0 \end{array}$$

1	S. 2) 1.3	S. 5) 2.3	1. 2) .23
2			
3			
4	2. 5) 3.1	3. 5) 0.2	4. 5) 0.3
5			
6			
7	5. 5) .32	6. 20) 2.4	7. 2) 1.9
8			
9	8. 5) 2.09	9. 2) .37	10. 4) .54
10			
Score			

56

A car can travel 53.2 miles in one hour. If the car is driven at this rate for 4 hours, how far will it have gone?

Problem Solving

Review Exercises	Speed Drills

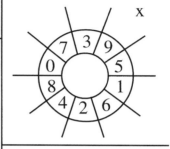

1. $3\overline{)\,2.4}$ **2.** $2\overline{)\,7.3}$

3. $5\overline{)\,.13}$ **4.** $2\overline{)\,.012}$

To change a fraction to a decimal, divide the numerator by the denominator. Add as many zeroes as needed.

Examples:

$$\frac{1}{4} = 4\overline{)\,1.00} \quad \begin{array}{r} .25 \\ \underline{-8\downarrow} \\ 20 \\ \underline{-20} \\ 0 \end{array}$$

$$\frac{1}{5} = 5\overline{)\,1.0} \quad \begin{array}{r} .2 \\ \underline{-10} \\ 0 \end{array}$$

Helpful Hints

Change each of the following fractions to a decimal.

S. $\dfrac{1}{2}$ **S.** $\dfrac{2}{5}$ **1.** $\dfrac{1}{4}$

2. $\dfrac{3}{5}$ **3.** $\dfrac{3}{4}$ **4.** $\dfrac{1}{8}$

5. $\dfrac{4}{5}$ **6.** $\dfrac{1}{5}$ **7.** $\dfrac{4}{20}$

8. $\dfrac{8}{20}$ **9.** $\dfrac{7}{10}$ **10.** $\dfrac{3}{8}$

1	
2	
3	
4	
5	
6	
7	
8	
9	
10	
Score	

Problem Solving | A boy earned 60 dollars by washing cars. He put $\frac{1}{3}$ of his money into a savings account. How much did he save?

57

Speed Drills	Review Exercises

+

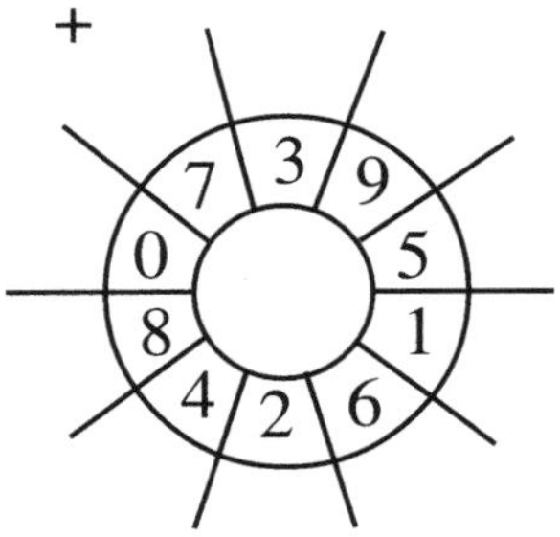

x

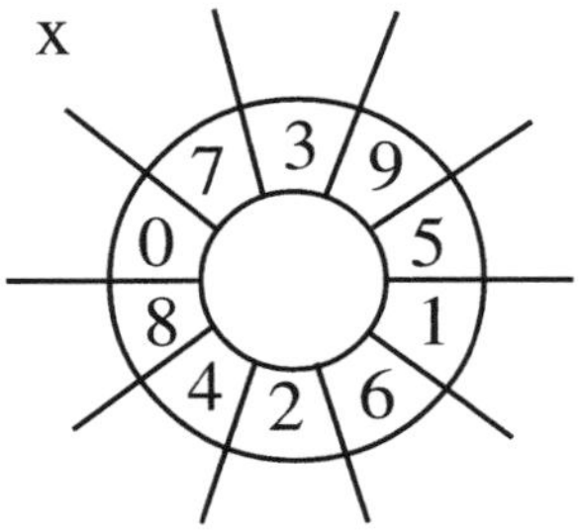

1. $2\overline{)4.8}$ 2. $3\overline{).09}$

3. $2\overline{).23}$ 4. change $\frac{2}{5}$ to a decimal

Helpful Hints

Use what you have learned to solve the following problems.

* Add as many zeroes as necessary.
* Placeholders may be necessary.
* Place decimal points properly.

1	
2	S. $2\overline{)2.4}$ S. $6\overline{).24}$ 1. $3\overline{)66.9}$
3	
4	2. $5\overline{).23}$ 3. $5\overline{)3.2}$ 4. $3\overline{)2.31}$
5	
6	
7	5. $5\overline{).16}$ 6. $5\overline{).3}$ 7. Change $\frac{4}{5}$ to a decimal.
8	
9	8. $6\overline{)3.24}$ 9. $4\overline{)1.324}$ 10. Change $\frac{1}{4}$ to a decimal.
10	
Score	

58   John weighed 120.5 pounds in January. In June, after track season, he had lost 3.25 pounds. How much did he weigh in June?

Problem Solving

1.   2.34
       .3
   + 2.13

2.   3.2 + 2 + 1.3 =

3.   18.6
    + .73

4.   7.23
    - 2.12

5.   5.1
    -   2.23

6.   5 - 2.33 =

7.   2.3
    x   3

8.   2.43
    x   4

9.   2.42
    x   3

10.   42.3
    x   .5

11.   3.4
    x   2.1

12.   3.12
    x   4.3

13. $2 \overline{)\ 2.46}$

14. $3 \overline{)\ 3.63}$

15. $2 \overline{)\ .15}$

16. $5 \overline{)\ .115}$

17. $5 \overline{)\ 3.25}$

18. $3 \overline{)\ .123}$

19. Change $\frac{1}{5}$ to a decimal.

20. Change $\frac{4}{5}$ to a decimal.

1	
2	
3	
4	
5	
6	
7	
8	
9	
10	
11	
12	
13	
14	
15	
16	
17	
18	
19	
20	

Speed Drills

+

x

Review Exercises

1.
$$\frac{2}{3}$$
$$-\frac{1}{2}$$

2.
$$\frac{1}{2}$$
$$+\frac{1}{4}$$

3. $\frac{3}{5} \times \frac{10}{11} =$

4. $\frac{1}{3} \div \frac{1}{2} =$

A ratio compares two numbers or groups of objects.

Example: ○ ○ ○   For every 3 circles
             □ □ □ □   there are 4 squares.

The ratio can be written in the following ways:

3 to 4,   3 : 4,   and $\frac{3}{4}$ Each of these is read as "3 to 4."

Ratios are often written in fraction form.

Helpful Hints

	1
	2
	3
	4
	5
	6
	7
	8
	9
	10
	Score

Write each of the following ratios as a fraction:

S.   5 nickels to 3 dimes   S.   9 horses to 4 cows

1.   7 to 2   2.   6 children to 5 adults

3.   4 books to 3 pencils   4.   5 bats to 3 balls

5.   6 : 5   6.   8 to 3

7.   7 dimes to 3 pennies   8.   6 chairs to 4 desks

9.   4 cats to 8 dogs   10. 9 : 3

60

John's car gets 13 miles to a gallon of gas. If he has only four gallons left in the tank, how far can he go before he runs out?

Problem Solving

Review Exercises	Speed Drills

1. 700 - 26 =

2. 314
   x   5

3.   23
     243
   + 542

4. 4) 804

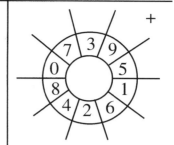

Equal ratios show the same comparison.

The ratio of squares to circles is: $\frac{4}{6}$ or $\frac{2}{3}$

Two equal ratios can be written as a proportion: $\frac{4}{6} = \frac{2}{3}$

Proportions can be solved the same way as finding equivalent fractions. Examples:

$\frac{2}{3} = \frac{?}{6} \quad 4 \qquad \frac{2}{3} \times \frac{2}{2} = \frac{4}{6} \qquad \frac{8}{10} = \frac{?}{5} \quad 4 \quad 2\overline{)\frac{8}{10}} = \frac{4}{5}$

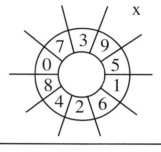

Helpful Hints

Solve each proportion by multiplying or dividing.

1	
2	
3	
4	
5	
6	
7	
8	
9	
10	
Score	

S. $\frac{2}{4} = \frac{?}{8}$

S. $\frac{6}{4} = \frac{?}{2}$

1. $\frac{4}{3} = \frac{?}{6}$

2. $\frac{5}{2} = \frac{10}{?}$

3. $\frac{2}{7} = \frac{?}{21}$

4. $\frac{6}{2} = \frac{?}{1}$

5. $\frac{3}{4} = \frac{?}{8}$

6. $\frac{5}{2} = \frac{?}{4}$

7. $\frac{3}{4} = \frac{6}{?}$

8. $\frac{3}{10} = \frac{?}{20}$

9. $\frac{3}{4} = \frac{?}{12}$

10. $\frac{5}{2} = \frac{?}{6}$

Problem Solving Five boys did a chore for a neighbor and earned a total of $7.25. How much money did each boy get when they divided it equally?

61

Speed Drills	Review Exercises

Speed Drills

+

x

Helpful Hints

Review Exercises

1. Write 7 to 2 as a fraction

2. Write as a ratio in three forms.

3. $\frac{2}{3} = \frac{?}{6}$

4. $\frac{6}{4} = \frac{3}{?}$

Percent means "per hundred" or "hundredths." If a fraction is expressed as hundredths, it can easily be written as a percent.

Examples:

$$\frac{7}{100} = 7\% \qquad \frac{16}{100} = 16\% \qquad \frac{3}{10} = \frac{30}{100} = 30\%$$

*Be sure to change tenths to hundredths.

	1
	2
	3
	4
	5
	6
	7
	8
	9
	10
	Score

Change each of the following to percents.

S. $\frac{12}{100} =$ S. $\frac{9}{10} =$ 1. $\frac{6}{100} =$ 2. $\frac{23}{100} =$

3. $\frac{2}{10} =$ 4. $\frac{34}{100} =$ 5. $\frac{75}{100} =$ 6. $\frac{1}{100} =$

7. $\frac{7}{10} =$ 8. $\frac{15}{100} =$ 9. $\frac{80}{100} =$ 10. $\frac{62}{100} =$

62   A woman bought 3 chairs. If each chair weighed 12.3 pounds, what was the total weight of the chairs?

Problem Solving

Review Exercises	Speed Drills

1. $\dfrac{7}{100} =$ _____%   2. $\dfrac{4}{10} =$ _____%

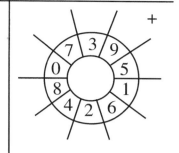

3. $\dfrac{1}{2}$ of $\dfrac{4}{5} =$ 4. Find the difference between 9.6 and 3.4.

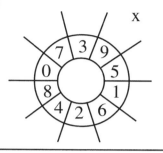

Decimals can easily be changed to percents
   * Move the decimal point twice to the right and
     add a percent symbol.
   * Be sure to change tenths to hundredths.

"Hundredths" = percent
Example: .15 = 15%   .3 = .30 = 30%

Helpful
Hints

Change each of the following to percents.

S. .12   S. .7   1. .32   2. .02

3. .5   4. .05   5. .6   6. .44

7. .79   8. .4   9. .33   10. .8

1	
2	
3	
4	
5	
6	
7	
8	
9	
10	
Score	

Problem Solving   There are 4 quarts in a gallon. How many quarts are there in 3 gallons?

63

Speed Drills	Review Exercises

1. Reduce $\frac{6}{8}$ to its lowest terms.

2. Change $\frac{7}{3}$ to a mixed numeral.

3. $\frac{3}{4} = \frac{6}{?}$

4. 7

   $- 2\frac{1}{3}$

Percents can be easily expressed as decimals and fractions.

Examples:

$25\% = .25 = \frac{25}{100}$

$8\% = .08 = \frac{8}{100}$

$30\% = .30 = \frac{30}{100}$

Helpful Hints

	1	
	2	
	3	
	4	
	5	
	6	
	7	
	8	
	9	
	10	
	Score	

Change each percent to a decimal and a fraction.

S. 12% = .   = —   S. 4% = .   = —   1. 16% = .   = —

2. 6% = .   = —   3. 75% = .   = —   4. 40% = .   = —

5. 1% = .   = —   6. 45% = .   = —   7. 12% = .   = —

8. 5% = .   = —   9. 50% = .   = —   10. 13% = .   = —

64   75% of the students at Pine School take the bus. What fraction of the students take the bus?   Problem Solving

Review Exercises	Speed Drills

1. $2 \overline{)\ 4.8}$ 2. Change $\frac{2}{5}$ to a decimal.

3.   .24   4.   321
   x   .6   x   .23

To find the percent   Find 3% of 60   Find 40% of 35
of a number, change   .03 x 60   .4 x 35
the percent to a
decimal and multiply.   60   35
                              x .03   x   .4
       Examples: 180   14.0
                                 00
                                1.80

S. Find 2% of 60.   S. Find 30% of 40.   1. Find 3% of 52.

2. Find 40% of 35.   3. Find 4% of 30.   4. Find 40% of 30.

5. Find 12% of 40.   6. Find 3% of 200.   7. Find 30% of 200.

8. Find 12% of 50.   9. Find 20% of 8.   10. Find 2% of 80.

Speed Drills

Helpful Hints

1	
2	
3	
4	
5	
6	
7	
8	
9	
10	
Score	

Problem Solving A gasoline tank holds $5\frac{1}{2}$ gallons. If $3\frac{1}{5}$ gallons have been used, then how many gallons are left in the tank?

65

Speed Drills	Review Exercises

+

1. Find 13% of 24.

2. Change $\frac{4}{5}$ to a decimal

3. Change 3% to a decimal.

4. Find 20% of 60.

x

When finding the percent of a number in a word problem, you can change the percent to a decimal. Always express your answer in a short phrase or sentence.

Example:

A team played 60 games and won 75% of them. How many games did they win?

Find 75% of 60
.75 x 60

$$\begin{array}{r} 60 \\ \times\ .75 \\ \hline 300 \\ 420 \\ \hline 45.00 \end{array}$$

Answer: The team won 45 games.

Helpful Hints

	1
	2
	3
	4
	5
	6
	7
	8

S. George took a test with 20 problems. If he got 15% of the problems correct, how many problems did he get correct?

S. If 6% of the 500 students enrolled in a school are absent, then how many students are absent?

1. A worker earned 80 dollars and put 30% of it into the bank. How many dollars did he put into the bank?

2. A car costs $4,000. If Mr. Smith has saved 20% of this amount, how much did he save?

3. Steve took a test with 30 problems. If he go 30% of the problems correct, how many problems did he get correct?

4. A family's monthly income is $3,000. If 20% of this amount is spent on food, how many dollars are spent on food?

5. There are 40 students in a class. If 60% of the class are boys, then how many boys are in the class?

6. A house that costs $80,000 requires a 20% down payment. How many dollars are required for the down payment?

7. If a car costs $6,000 and loses 30% of its value in one year, how much value will the car lose in one year?

8. A coat is priced $50. If the sales tax is 7% of the price, how much is the sales tax?

Score	

66

A train traveled 83.5 miles per hour. At this rate, how far would it travel in 2 hours?

Problem Solving

Review Exercises	Speed Drills

1. Find 5% of 60.

2.
$$\begin{array}{r} 43 \\ \times\ 32 \\ \hline \end{array}$$

3.   24 + 143 + 25 =

4.
$$\begin{array}{r} 705 \\ -\ 324 \\ \hline \end{array}$$

+

7 3 9
0   5
8   1
4 2 6

To change a fraction to a percent first change the fraction to a decimal, then change the decimal to a percent. Move the decimal twice to the right and add a percent symbol.

x

7 3 9
0   5
8   1
4 2 6

Examples: $\dfrac{2}{5}$
$$\begin{array}{r} .40 = 40\% \\ 5\ )\ \overline{2.0} \\ -2\ 0 \\ \hline 0 \end{array}$$

$\dfrac{2}{8} = \dfrac{1}{4}$
$$\begin{array}{r} .25 = 25\% \\ 4\ )\ \overline{1.00} \\ -\ 8\downarrow \\ \hline 20 \\ -\ 20 \\ \hline 0 \end{array}$$

*Sometimes the fraction can be reduced

Helpful Hints

Change each of the following to percents.

S. $\dfrac{1}{2} =$

S. $\dfrac{6}{10} =$

1. $\dfrac{4}{20} =$

2. $\dfrac{4}{10} =$

3. $\dfrac{3}{12} =$

4. $\dfrac{5}{10} =$

5. $\dfrac{3}{10} =$

6. $\dfrac{15}{20} =$

7. $\dfrac{6}{12} =$

8. $\dfrac{4}{16} =$

9. $\dfrac{2}{4} =$

10. $\dfrac{3}{15} =$

1	
2	
3	
4	
5	
6	
7	
8	
9	
10	
Score	

Problem Solving | John earned 30 dollars. If he put 20% of it into the bank, how much did he put into the bank?

67

Speed Drills	Review Exercises

Speed Drills

+

7 3 9
0   5
8   1
4 2 6

x

7 3 9
0   5
8   1
4 2 6

Helpful Hints

Review Exercises

1.   7.12
    x   3

2.   7.6
    - 2.32

3.   2.64
    + 3.37

4.   5) .15

When finding the percent, first write a fraction, change the fraction to a decimal, then change the decimal to a percent.

Examples:

2 is what % of 8?

3 is what % of 5?

$\frac{2}{8} = \frac{1}{4}$ 4) 1.00 → .25 = 25%

$\frac{3}{5}$ 5) 3.0 → .60 = 60%
    - 3 0
       0

    - 8↓
       20
    - 20
       0

1	
2	S. 2 is what % of 5? S. 2 is what % of 10? 1. 4 is what % of 5?
3	
4	
5	2. 3 is what % of 6? 3. 8 is what % of 10? 4. 4 is what % of 16?
6	
7	5. 5 is what % of 10? 6. 3 is what % of 15? 7. 2 is what % of 5?
8	
9	
10	8. 3 is what % of 12? 9. 2 is what % of 4? 10. 5 is what % of 25?
Score	

68

A man had 75 dollars. One day he spent 12 dollars. The next day he earned 8 dollars. How much money does he have now?

Problem Solving

Review Exercises	Speed Drills

1.   Find 12% of 42.   2.   Change $\frac{2}{5}$ to a decimal

3.   Find 30% of 50.   4. $3 \overline{)\,.18}$

+

When finding the percent, first write a fraction, change the fraction to a decimal, then change the decimal to a percent.

Example:

A team played 8 games and won 2 of them. What percent of the games did they win?

2 is what % of 8?

$\frac{2}{8} = \frac{1}{4}$

$$4 \overline{)\,1.00}$$
$$\underline{-\ 8\downarrow}$$
$$20$$
$$\underline{-\ 20}$$
$$0$$

$.25 = 25\%$

They won 25% of the games.

x

Helpful Hints

S. A test had 15 questions. If Sam got 5 questions correct, what percent did he get correct?

1. On a spelling test with 12 words, Susan got 3 correct. What percent of the words did she get correct?

3. A team played 5 games and won 3 of them. What percent did they win?

5. $\frac{2}{5}$ of a class was present at school. What percent of the class was present?

7. A team played 12 games and lost 3 games. What percent of the games played did it lose?

9. On a math test with 10 questions, Jill got 9 of them correct. What percent did she get correct?

S. In a class of 15 students, 3 are girls. What percent of the class is girls?

2. A worker earned 20 dollars. If she put 5 dollars into a savings account, what percent of her earnings did she put into a savings account?

4. A quarterback threw 25 passes and 20 were caught. What percent of the passes were caught?

6. A class has an enrollment of 20 students. If 2 are absent, what percent are absent?

8. A class has 20 students. If 8 of them are boys, what percent are boys?

10. A pitcher threw 8 pitches. If 4 of them were strikes, what percent were strikes?

1	
2	
3	
4	
5	
6	
7	
8	
9	
10	
Score	

Problem Solving | There are 20 questions on a test. If a student got 80% of them correct, how many questions did he get correct?

69

Speed Drills	Review Exercises

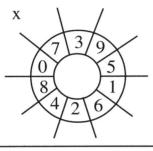

1. Change $\frac{7}{100}$ to a percent.   2. Change $\frac{9}{10}$ to a percent.

3. Change .03 to a percent.   4. Change .7 to a percent.

Helpful Hints

Use what you have learned to solve the problem. Examples:	Find 12% of 60 .12 x 60 60 x .12 120 60 7.20	3 is what % of 12? $\frac{3}{12} = \frac{1}{4}$ 4) 1.00 → .25 = 25% - 8↓ 20 - 20 0

	1			
	2	S. Find 20% of 30.	S. 2 is what % of 8?	1. Find 3% of 60.
	3			
	4	2. Find 12% of 65.	3. 3 is what % of 5?	4. 4 is what % of 8?
	5			
	6			
	7	5. Find 30% of 60	6. Find 5% of 16	7. 5 is what % of 25?
	8			
	9	8. Find 15% of 40.	9. Find 50% of 30.	10. 4 is what % of 5?
	10			
	Score			

There were 30 problems on a test. If a student got 80% of them correct, how many problems did he get correct? | Problem Solving

Review Exercises

Speed Drills

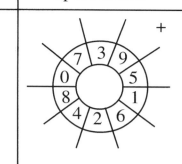

1. $\dfrac{5}{6}$

  $-\dfrac{1}{6}$

2. $\dfrac{3}{8}$

  $+\dfrac{1}{8}$

3. $\dfrac{3}{5}$ x $\dfrac{10}{11}$ =

4. $\dfrac{2}{3}$ ÷ $\dfrac{1}{3}$ =

Use what you have learned to solve the problem. Examples:

A farmer has 20 cows. If he sells 40% of them, how many does he sell?

In a class of 20 students, 5 are girls. What percent are girls?

5 is what % of 20?

Find 40% of 20
.4 x 20

$$\begin{array}{r} 20 \\ \times\ .4 \\ \hline 8.0 \end{array}$$

He sold 8 cows.

$\dfrac{5}{20} = \dfrac{1}{4}$

25% are girls.

$$\begin{array}{r} 25 = 25\% \\ 4\,\overline{)\,1.00} \\ -\ \underline{8\downarrow} \\ 20 \\ -\ \underline{20} \\ 0 \end{array}$$

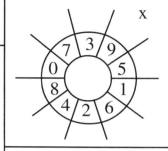

Helpful
Hints

S. A test has 40 problems. A student got 30% of them correct. How many problems did he get correct?

S. Sue has finished 3 problems on a test. If there are 12 problems on the test, what percent has she finished?

1. A ranch has 500 acres of land. If 60% of the land is used for grazing, then how many acres are used for grazing?

2. A player took 5 shots. If he made 3 of them, what percent did he make?

3. A man earned 20 dollars and spent 60% of it. How much did he spend?

4. A test has 20 questions. If Jane got 15 correct, what percent did she get correct?

5. 4 is what percent of 5?

6. Find 12% of 40.

7. There are 400 students in a school. If 60% eat cafeteria food, how many students eat cafeteria food?

8. A baseball team played 5 games and won 3. What percent did they win?

9. A car costs $6,000. If a down payment of 20% is required, how much is the down payment?

10. 10 players tried out for a team. If only 6 made the team, what percent made the team?

1	
2	
3	
4	
5	
6	
7	
8	
9	
10	
Score	

Problem
Solving

A man can run 6 miles per hour. At this rate how far can he run in $1\frac{1}{2}$ hours?

Reviewing Ratios, Proportions, and Percent

Write numbers 1 and 2 as a ratio expressed in fraction form.

1.   7 nickels to 2 dimes   2.   9 to 4

For numbers 3 and 4 solve each proportion.

3. $\dfrac{4}{5} = \dfrac{?}{10}$ 4. $\dfrac{3}{4} = \dfrac{9}{?}$

Change numbers 5 through 8 to a percent.

5. $\dfrac{17}{100} =$ 6. $\dfrac{7}{10} =$ 7. $.19 =$ 8. $.6 =$

Change numbers 9 through 11 to a decimal and a fraction.

9. $6\% = .$ $=$ $-$ 10. $15\% = .$ $=$ $-$

11. $80\% = .$ $=$ $-$

12.   Find 4% of 60.   13.   Find 30% of 40.

14.   6 is what % of 8?   15.   3 is what % of 5?

16.   Change $\dfrac{1}{5}$ to a percent.   17.   Change $\dfrac{1}{4}$ to a percent.

18.   A man earned 40 dollars. If he put 20% of it into the bank, how much did he put into the bank?

19.   A woman baked 8 cakes. If she sold 6 of them, what percent did she sell?

20.   On a test with 20 questions, a student got 70% correct. How many questions did the student get correct?

	1
	2
	3
	4
	5
	6
	7
	8
	9
	10
	11
	12
	13
	14
	15
	16
	17
	18
	19
	20

Review Exercises	Speed Drills

1.   3.2 + .54 + 2.8 =   2.   7.6 – 5.8 =

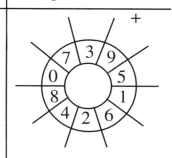

4.   1.64   3.   5) 3.0
      x .03

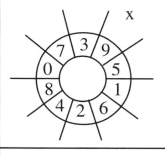

Geometric term:	Point	Line	Plane	Line Segment	Ray
Example:	• P	A B		A B	A B
Symbol:	P	$\overleftrightarrow{AB}$	plane ABC	$\overline{AB}$	$\overrightarrow{AB}$

Helpful
Hints

Use the figure to answer the following.

S. Name 2 points   S. Name 2 line segments

1. Name 2 lines   2. Name 2 rays

3. Name 2 points on $\overleftrightarrow{FD}$

4. Give another name for $\overleftrightarrow{AB}$

5. Give another name for $\overleftrightarrow{ED}$

6. Give another name for $\overleftrightarrow{AC}$

7. Name a line segment on $\overleftrightarrow{FD}$

8. Name 2 rays on $\overleftrightarrow{FE}$

9. Name a ray on $\overleftrightarrow{AC}$

10. What point is common to lines $\overleftrightarrow{FD}$ and $\overleftrightarrow{BE}$?

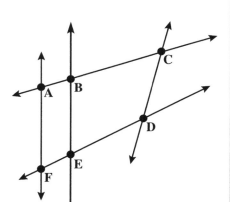

1	
2	
3	
4	
5	
6	
7	
8	
9	
10	
Score	

Problem Solving | If a factory can manufacture an engine in 2 hours, how long will it take to manufacture 10 engines?   73

Speed Drills	Review Exercises

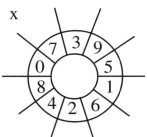

+

X

1. $\dfrac{3}{5}$
$+ \dfrac{4}{5}$

2. $\dfrac{3}{4}$
$- \dfrac{1}{4}$

3. $2 \times \dfrac{3}{4} =$

4. $3 \div \dfrac{3}{4} =$

Helpful Hints	Geometric term:	Parallel Lines	Intersecting Lines	Perpendiculat Lines	Angle Symbols

Geometric term: Parallel Lines   Intersecting Lines   Perpendiculat Lines   Angle   Symbols

Example: C   D   D   C   E   F   Vertex   ∠ DAC   ∠ CAD   ∠ A

1	
2	
3	
4	
5	
6	
7	
8	
9	
10	
Score	

Use the figure to answer the following.

S. Name 2 parallel lines

S. Name 2 perpendicular lines

1. Name a pair of intersecting lines

2. Name 2 angles

3. Name 2 angles that have B as their vertex

4. Name 2 angles that have H as their vertex

5. Name 2 lines   6. Name 2 line segments

7. Name 2 rays   8. Name a line segment on $\overleftrightarrow{BH}$

9. Name 2 lines that include point B

10. Give another name for △ JHI

74   Mary has a piece of cloth 123 yards long. How many pieces 3 yards long can she cut from it?   **Problem Solving**

Review Exercises	Speed Drills

1. 6 is what% of 8?

2. Find 12% of 80.

3. A man had 300 cows and decided to sell 20% of them. How many cows did he sell?

4. Sue took a test with 20 problems. If she got 12 of the problems correct, then what percent of the problems did she get correct?

right angle
measures 90°

acute angle
measures less than 90°

obtuse angle
measures more than 90°

straight angle
measures 180°

Helpful Hints

Use the figure to answer the following.

S. Name 2 right angles

S. Name 2 acute angles

1. Name 2 obtuse angles

2. Name 2 straight angles

3. What kind of angle is △ IJG?

4. What kind of angle is △ EDB?

5. What kind of angle is △ GBD?

6. What kind of angle is △ GJK?

7. Name an acute angle which has J as its vertex.

8. Name an obtuse angle that has D as its vertex.

9. Name a right angle which has B as its vertex.

10. Name a straight angle which has D as its vertex.

1	
2	
3	
4	
5	
6	
7	
8	
9	
10	
Score	

Problem Solving A rope is 1.7 meters long. If a man wants to cut it into 5 pieces of equal length, how long will each piece be?

75

Speed Drills	Review Exercises

+

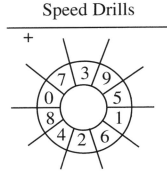

x

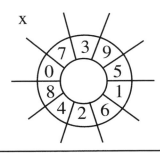

Helpful Hints

1. Change $\dfrac{9}{7}$ to a mixed numeral.

2. Change $2\dfrac{1}{2}$ to an improper fraction

3. Express $\dfrac{8}{10}$ in its lowest terms.

4. $1\dfrac{1}{2}$ x $1\dfrac{1}{3}$ =

To use a protractor, follow these rules:
1. Place the center point of the proctractor on the vertex.
2. Place the zero mark on one edge of the angle.
3. Read the number where the other side of the angle crosses the proctractor.
4. If the angle is acute, use the smaller number. If the angle is obtuse, use the larger number.

1	Use the figure to answer the questions. Classify the angle as right, acute, obtuse, or straight. Then tell how many degrees the angle measures.
2	
3	
4	
5	
6	
7	
8	
9	
10	
Score	

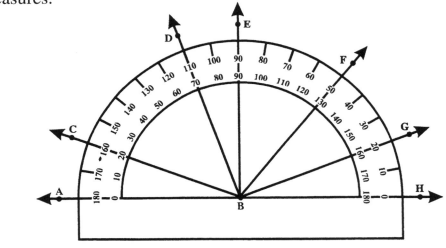

S. ∠HBG   S. ∠DHB   1. ∠EBH   2. ∠CBH
3. ∠GBH   4. ∠DBA   5. ∠ABF   6. ∠FBH
7. ∠ABH   8. ∠ABG   9. ∠EBA   10. ∠FBA

76   50 students took a social studies test and 80% received a passing grade. How many students received a passing grade?

Problem Solving

Review Exercises	Speed Drills

1. Change $\frac{4}{5}$ to a percent.   2. Change .9 to a percent.

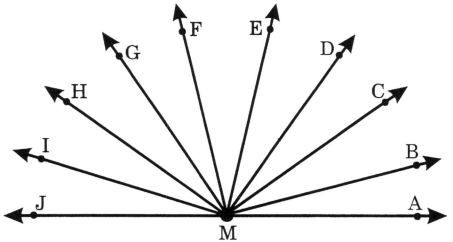

3. Find 4% of 65.   4. 6 is what percent of 8?

To use a protractor, follow these rules:
1. Place the center point of the proctractor on the vertex.
2. Place the zero mark on one edge of the angle.
3. Read the number where the other side of the angle crosses the proctractor.
4. If the angle is acute, use the smaller number. If the angle is obtuse, use the larger number.

Helpful
Hints

With a protractor, measure the indicated angle in the figure. Tell the number of degrees. Also, classify the angle as acute, right, obtuse, or straight.

1	
2	
3	
4	
5	
6	
7	
8	
9	
10	
Score	

S. ∡AMC S. ∡EMA 1. ∡DMA   2. ∡FMJ   3. ∡FMA
4. ∡DMJ   5. ∡EMA 6. ∡CMA   7. ∡HMJ   8. ∡GMJ
9. ∡IMA 10.   ∡IMJ

Problem
Solving

There are 645 seats in an auditorium. If 379 of the seats are occupied, how many seats are empty?

77

Speed Drills	Review Exercises

+

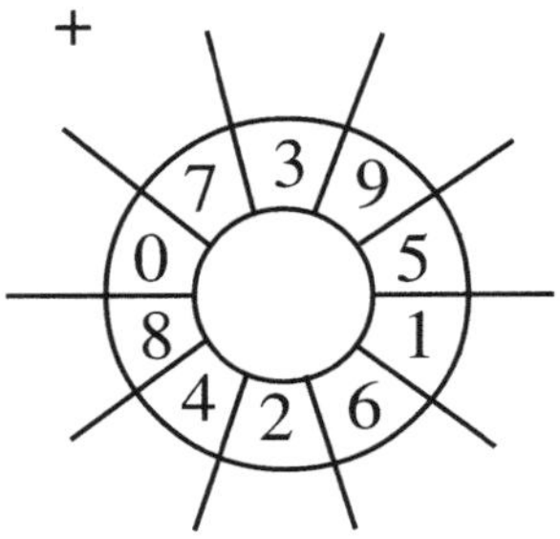

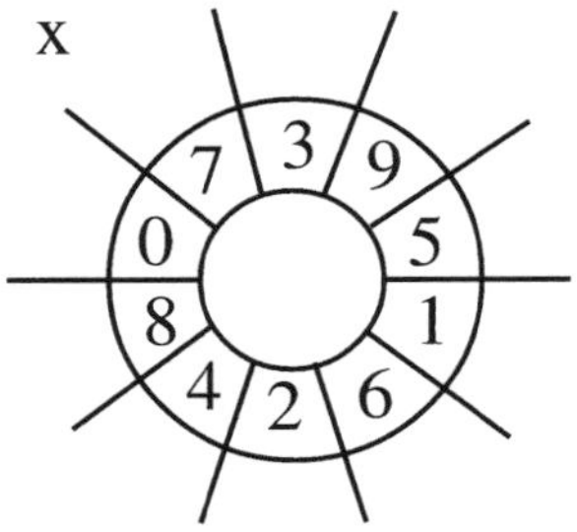

1. Name and classify this angle.

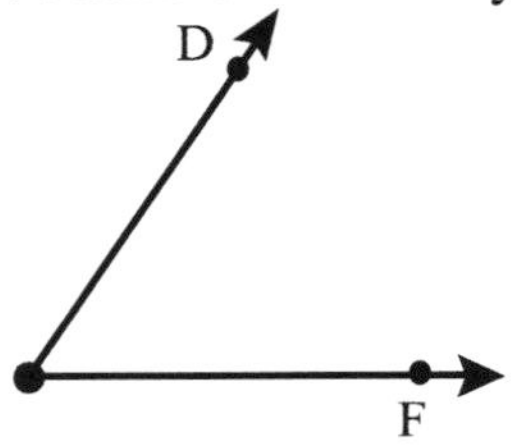

2. Name and classify this angle.

x

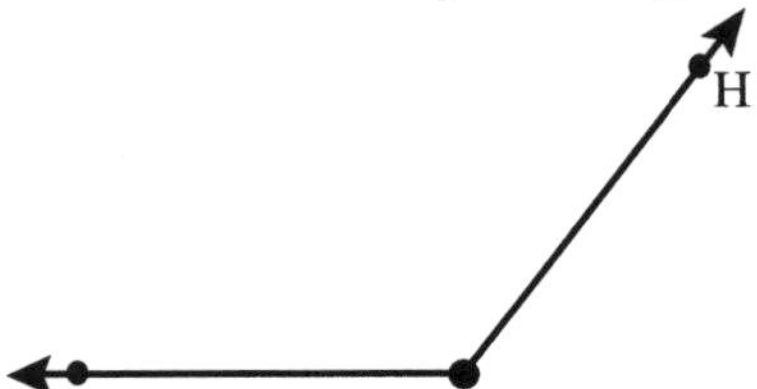

3. Name and classify this angle.

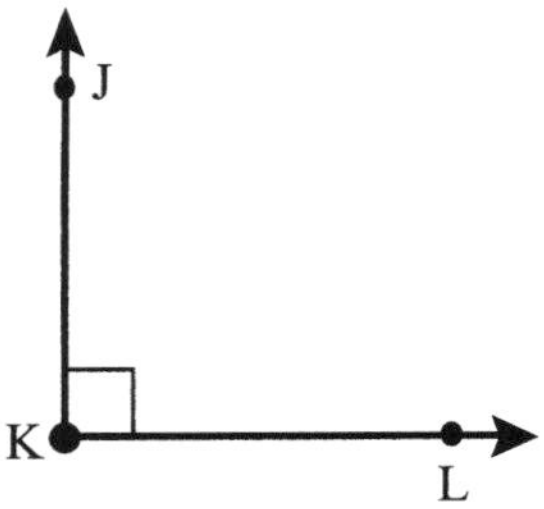

4. What kind of lines are these?

Helpful Hints	Polygons are closed figures made up of line segments.	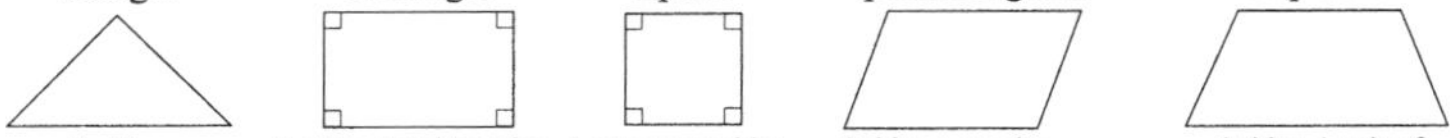 triangle 3 sides	rectangle 4 sides, 4 right angles	square 4 congruent sides, 4 right angles	parallelogram 4 sides, opposite sides parallel	trapezoid 4 sides, 1 pair of parallel sides

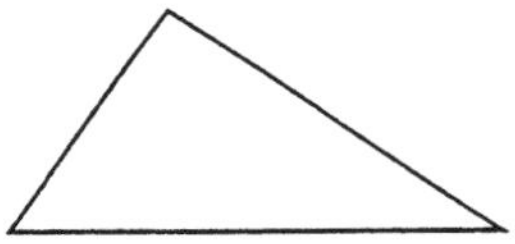

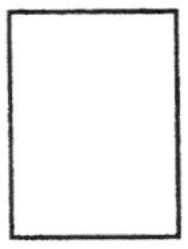

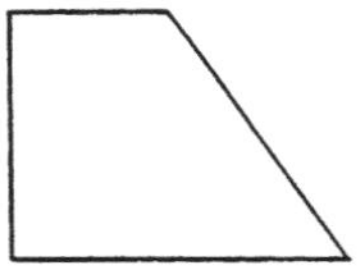

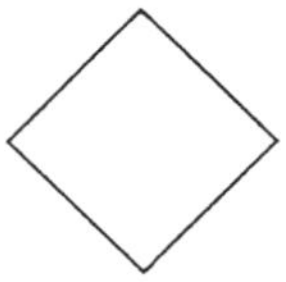

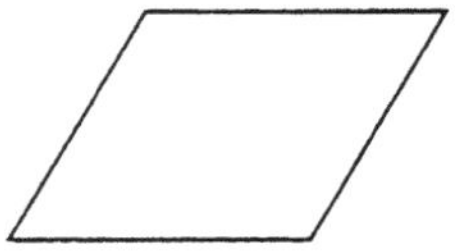

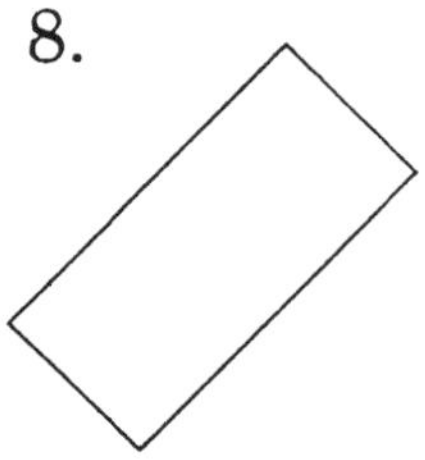

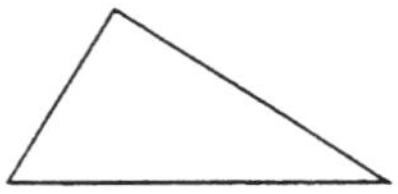

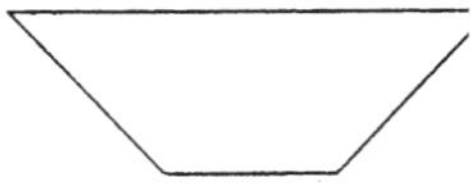

1	Name each polygon. Some may have more than one name.
2	S. S. 1. 2.
3	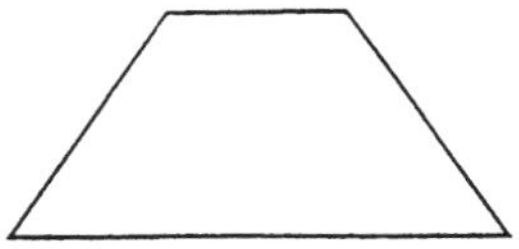
4	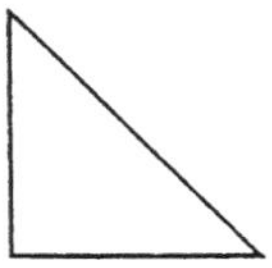
5	3. 4. 5. 6.
6	
7	
8	7. 8. 9. 10.
9	
10	
Score	

A man earned $3.75 per hour. How much was his pay if he worked 4 hours?

Problem Solving

Review Exercises	Speed Drills

1. 3) 758

2. 62
    x 50

3. 732
    46
    + 322

4. 723
    - 435

+

x

Triangles can be classified by sides and angles.

Sides

equilateral — 3 congruent sides

scalene — no congruent sides

isoceles — 2 congruent sides

Angles

acute — 3 acute angles

right — 1 right angle

obtuse — 1 obtuse angle

Helpful Hints

Classify each triangle by its sides and angles.

1	
2	
3	
4	
5	
6	
7	
8	
9	
10	
Score	

S. sides: _____ angles: _____
40° 4 5 50° 3

S. sides: _____ angles: _____
60° 7 7 60° 60° 7

1. sides: _____ angles: _____
40° 12 7 120° 20° 9

2. sides: _____ angles: _____
80° 7 7 50° 50° 9

3. sides: _____ angles: _____
45° 8 6 45° 6

4. sides: _____ angles: _____
70° 7 3 80° 30° 6

5. sides: _____ angles: _____

6. sides: _____ angles: _____
8 30° 5 40° 110° 3

7. sides: _____ angles: _____
60° 5 3 30° 4

8. sides: _____ angles: _____

9. sides: _____ angles: _____
60° 9 ft. 9 ft. 60° 60° 9 ft.

10. sides: _____ angles: _____
45° 45°

Problem Solving	Buses hold 60 people, How many buses are needed for 143 people?

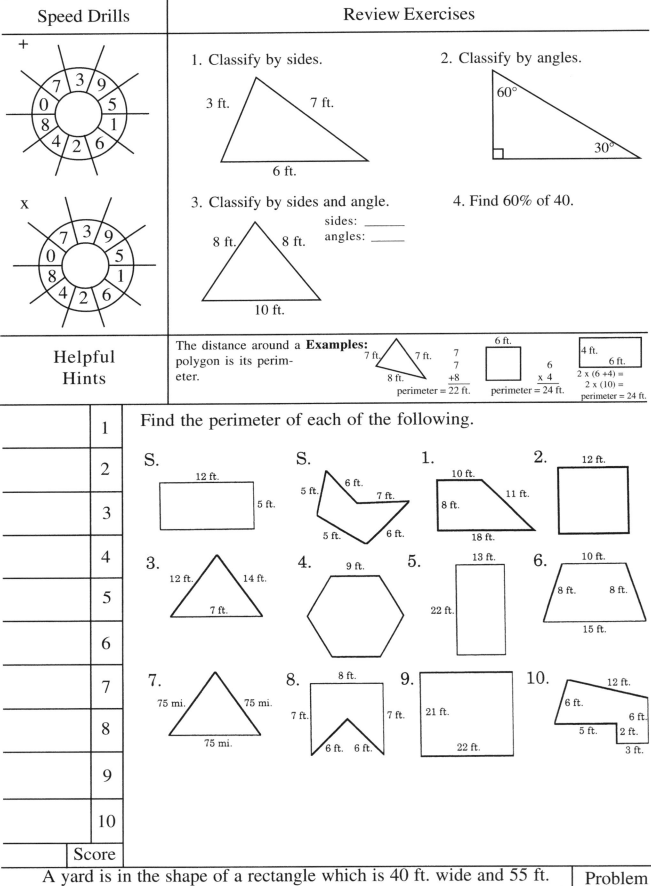

Speed Drills

+

x

Review Exercises

1. Classify by sides.

3 ft.   7 ft.

6 ft.

2. Classify by angles.

60°

30°

3. Classify by sides and angle.

8 ft.   8 ft.

10 ft.

sides: _____

angles: _____

4. Find 60% of 40.

Helpful Hints

The distance around a polygon is its perimeter.

Examples:

7 ft.   7 ft.

8 ft.

7
7
+8
perimeter = 22 ft.

6 ft.

6
x 4
perimeter = 24 ft.

4 ft.
6 ft.

2 x (6 +4) =
2 x (10) =
perimeter = 24 ft.

Find the perimeter of each of the following.

S.
12 ft.
5 ft.

S.
5 ft.   6 ft.
7 ft.
5 ft.   6 ft.

1.
10 ft.
8 ft.   11 ft.
18 ft.

2.
12 ft.

3.
12 ft.   14 ft.
7 ft.

4.
9 ft.

5.
13 ft.
22 ft.

6.
10 ft.
8 ft.   8 ft.
15 ft.

7.
75 mi.   75 mi.
75 mi.

8.
8 ft.
7 ft.   7 ft.
6 ft.   6 ft.

9.
21 ft.
22 ft.

10.
12 ft.
6 ft.
5 ft.   2 ft.   6 ft.
3 ft.

	1
	2
	3
	4
	5
	6
	7
	8
	9
	10
	Score

80

A yard is in the shape of a rectangle which is 40 ft. wide and 55 ft. long. How many feet of fence will it take to go all the way around the yard? (Hint: Draw a sketch.)

Problem Solving

Review Exercises

1. Find the perimeter.

5 ft. | 16 ft. |

2. Find the perimeter.

14 ft. | |

3. 6 is what % of 30?

4.
$$\frac{3}{4}$$
$$-\frac{1}{3}$$

These are
the parts
of a circle.

chord
diameter
radius
center

* The length of the diameter is
twice that of the radius.

Use the figure to answer the following.

Circle A

G F
C E
D
B
A

Circle B

x
Y v
Z
o P
R S T

S. What part of the
circle is CE?

S. Name a chord in
circle B.

1. What part of circle
A is DF?

2. What part of circle
B is VT?

3. Name 2 radii in
circle A

4. Name 2 chords in
circle A

5. If the length of CE is 16 ft., what is the
length of CD?

6. Name the center
of circle B.

7. Name 2 chords in
circle B.

8. If PS in Circle B
is 8 ft., what is
the length of XS?

9. name 2 radii in
circle B.

10. Name a diameter
in circle B.

1	
2	
3	
4	
5	
6	
7	
8	
9	
10	
Score	

**Problem
Solving** A city is in the shape of a square. If its perimeter is 64 miles,
what is the length of each side of the city?

81

Speed Drills	Review Exercises

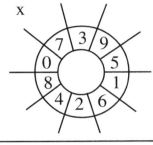

+

x

Helpful Hints

1.   233 + 15 + 6 =

2. $\frac{5}{8} = \frac{10}{?}$

3.   Find 20% of 60.

4.   3 is what % of 15?

The distance around a circle is called its circumference. The Greek letter π = pi = 3.14. To find the circumference, multiply π x diameter. C = π x d. Examples:

C = π x d
C = 3.14 x 6

6 ft.

3.14
x 6
18.84 ft

C = π x d
C = 3.14 x 12

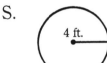
6 ft.

3.14
x 12
6 2 8
3 1 4 0
3 7.6 8 ft.

1	Find the circumference of each of the following. If there is no figure, draw a sketch.
2	
3	
4	
5	
6	
7	

S.

4 ft.

S.

4 ft.

1.

6 ft.

2.

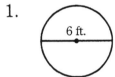
4 ft.

3. A circle with diameter 5 ft.

4. A circle with radius 1 ft.

5.

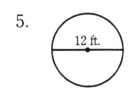
12 ft.

6.

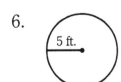
5 ft.

7. A circle with radius 2 ft.

Score

A garden is in the shape of a circle. If the diameter is 3 feet, how far is it all the way around the garden?

82

Problem Solving

Review Exercises	Speed Drills

1.   3.2
     x 6.1

2. $\frac{3}{4}$ x $1\frac{1}{3}$ =

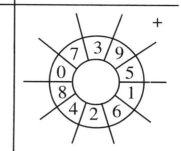

3. $2\frac{1}{2}$ x $1\frac{1}{5}$ =

4.   3 x 32. 5 =

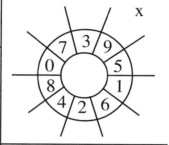

X

The number of square units needed to cover a region is called its area.

Examples:

area square = side x side   area rectangle = length x width

| s= 7 ft. | A= s x s   7 |
A= 7 x 7   x 7
49 sq. ft.

 w= 7 ft.   A= 1 x w   12
A= 12 x 7   x 7
l = 12 ft.   84 sq. ft.

Hint: 1. Start with formulas   2. Substitute values.   3. Solve the problem

Helpful
Hints

Find the following areas. If there is no figure, make a sketch.

S.   6 ft.
□

S.   12 ft.
6 ft.

1.   14 ft.
6 ft.

2.   20 ft.
□

3. A rectangle with
   length 12 ft. and
   width 11 ft.

4.   7 ft.
14 ft.

5.   16 ft.
6 ft.

6.   13 ft.

7. A square with sides
   11 ft.

1	
2	
3	
4	
5	
6	
7	

| Score | |

A floor is in the shape of a rectangle. The length is 14 feet and
the width is 13 feet. What is the perimeter of the floor?

Speed Drills	Review Exercises

+

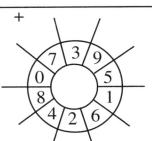

x

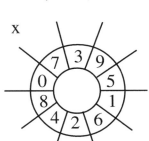

Helpful Hints

1. Find the area

16 ft.

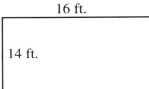

14 ft.

2. Find the area

16 ft.

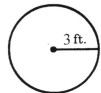

3. Find the circumference

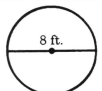

8 ft.

4. Find the circumference

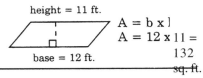

3 ft.

Area of a triangle = $\dfrac{\text{base x height}}{2} = \dfrac{b \times h}{2}$

Area parallelogram = base x height = b x h

Examples:

$A = \dfrac{b \times h}{2}$ height = 8 ft.   base = 7 ft.

$A = \dfrac{7 \times 8}{2} = \dfrac{56}{2}$

28 sq. ft.

2 ⌐ 56

height = 11 ft.   base = 12 ft.

A = b x l
A = 12 x 11 = 132 sq. ft.

	1
	2
	3
	4
	5
	6
	7

Find the following areas. If there is no figure, make a sketch.

S.
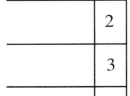
6 ft.
13 ft.

S.
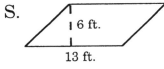
6 ft.
8 ft.

1.
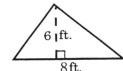
6 ft.
12 ft.

2.
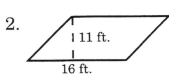
11 ft.
16 ft.

3. A triangle with base 5 ft. and height 6 ft.

4. A parallelogram with base 13 ft. and height 7 ft.

5.
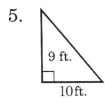
9 ft.
10ft.

6.
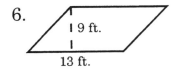
9 ft.
13 ft.

7.
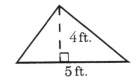
4 ft.
5 ft.

		Score	

84

A field is in the shape of a rectangle. If the length is 30 ft. and the width is 20 ft., what is the perimeter?

Problem Solving

Review Exercises

Speed Drills

1. Find the perimeter

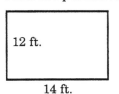
12 ft.
14 ft.

2. Find the area

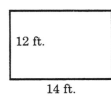
12 ft.
14 ft.

3. Find the circumference

6 ft.

4. Find the area

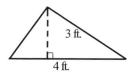
3 ft.
4 ft.

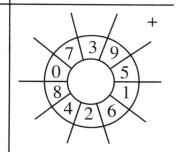
+

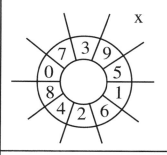
x

Remember these formulas.   For Areas: 1. Write formula 2. Substitute values 3. Solve problem

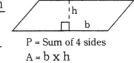

$A = \dfrac{b \times h}{2}$

C = Π x d

P = 4 x s
A = s x s

P = 2 (l + w)
A = l x w

P = Sum of all sides

P = Sum of 4 sides
A = b x h

Helpful Hints

Find the perimeter or circumference. Second, find the area. If there is no figure, make a sketch.

S.
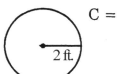
12 ft.
7 ft.

P =   A =

S.
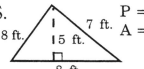
8 ft.   7 ft.   5 ft.
8 ft.

P =
A =

1.
12 ft.

P =
A =

2.
10 ft.
12 ft.

P =
A =

3.
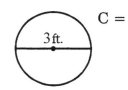
7 ft.   6 ft.
12 ft.

P =
A =

4.
3 ft.

C =

5.
2 ft.

C =

6.
10 ft.
6 ft.
8 ft.

P =
A =

7. A square with sides 8 ft.

P =   A =

1	
2	
3	
4	
5	
6	
7	

Score	

Problem Solving   A man wants to buy a tent which is in the shape of a rectangle. If the length is 18 feet and the width is 12 feet, what is the perimeter of the tent?

85

Speed Drills

+

x

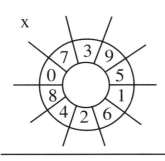

Helpful Hints

	1
	2
	3
	4
	5
	6
	7

	Score

Review Exercises

1. $\dfrac{3}{5}$

     $-\ \dfrac{1}{2}$

       —————

2. $\dfrac{2}{3}$

     $+\ \dfrac{1}{2}$

       —————

3. $3\dfrac{1}{2} \times 3 =$

4. $2\dfrac{1}{2} \div \dfrac{1}{2} =$

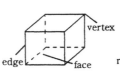
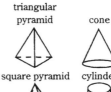

cube   triangular prism   triangular pyramid   cone

vertex   edge   face   rectangular prism   sphere   square pyramid   cylinder

cones and cylinders do not have straight edges

Identify the shape and the number of each part.

S.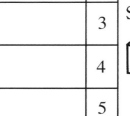
  name _____
  faces _____
  edges _____
  vertices _____

S.
  name _____
  faces _____
  edges _____
  vertices _____

1.
  name _____

2.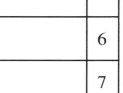
  name _____
  faces _____
  edges _____
  vertices _____

3.
  name _____

4.
  name _____
  faces _____
  edges _____
  vertices _____

5.
  name _____
  faces _____
  edges _____
  vertices _____

6.
  name _____

7. How many more faces does a cube have than a triangular prism?

Jill had $7.35 and spent $5.40. How much money does she have left?

Problem Solving

Use the figures to answer 1 - 8

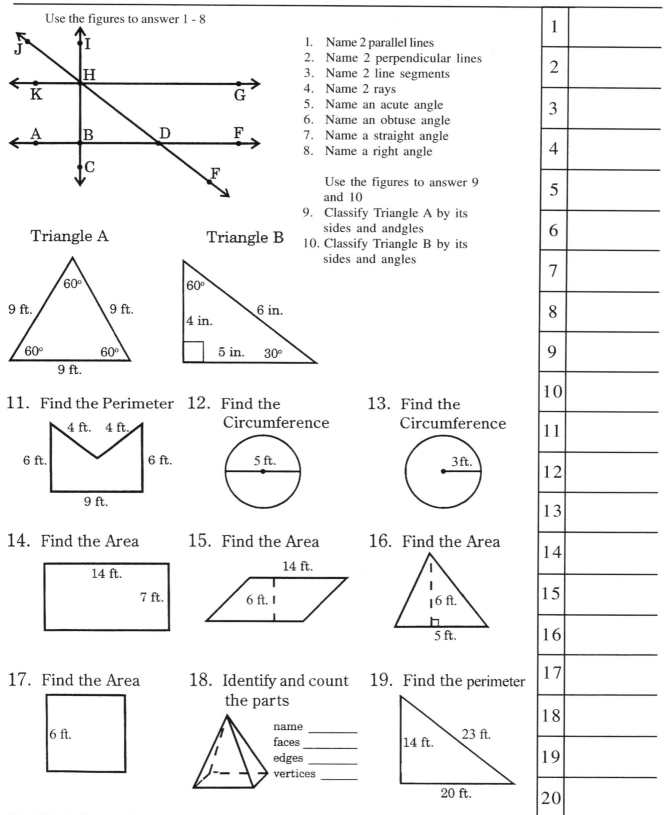

1. Name 2 parallel lines
2. Name 2 perpendicular lines
3. Name 2 line segments
4. Name 2 rays
5. Name an acute angle
6. Name an obtuse angle
7. Name a straight angle
8. Name a right angle

Use the figures to answer 9 and 10

9. Classify Triangle A by its sides and andgles
10. Classify Triangle B by its sides and angles

Triangle A

Triangle B

11. Find the Perimeter
12. Find the Circumference
13. Find the Circumference

14. Find the Area
15. Find the Area
16. Find the Area

17. Find the Area

18. Identify and count the parts

name _____
faces _____
edges _____
vertices _____

19. Find the perimeter

20. Find the perimeter of a square with sides of 16 feet.

1	
2	
3	
4	
5	
6	
7	
8	
9	
10	
11	
12	
13	
14	
15	
16	
17	
18	
19	
20	

Speed Drills	Review Exercises

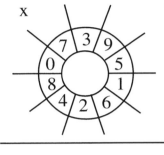

1.   703
    − 26

2. $\frac{2}{5}$
    + $\frac{1}{2}$

3.   3.6
    + 7.2

4.   Find 3% of 80.

Helpful Hints

The factor of a whole number is a whole number which divides into it evenly, without a remainder.
Example: Find all factors of 20.
1 x 20 = 20   2 x 10 = 20   4 x 5 = 20
So 1, 20, 2, 10, 4, 5 are all factors of 20.
The number 20 can be divided evenly by each of these factors.

	1
	2
	3
	4
	5
	6
	7
	8
	9
	10
	Score

Find all the factors of each number.

S. 10   S. 12   1. 15   2. 16

3. 9   4. 24   5. 30   6. 18

7. 8   8. 25   9. 17   10. 21

How much will a worker earn in 6 hours if he earns $4.50 per hour?

Problem Solving

Review Exercises	Speed Drills

1.   324
    x   6

2. $\frac{3}{4}$

    - $\frac{1}{4}$

3.   1.22
    x   .3

4.   Find the perimeter.
        7 ft.

        [   ] 3 ft.

The greatest common factor is the largest factor that two numbers have in common.

Example: Find the greatest common factor of 12 and 16

Find the factors   12: 1, 2, 3, ④ 6, 12
of each number: 16: 1, 2, ④ 8, 16
                4 is the greatest common factor.

Find the greatest common factor of each pair of numbers.

S. 8 and 10   S. 12 and 20   1. 6 and 8   2. 12 and 15

3. 15 and 20   4. 18 and 15   5. 16 and 20   6. 20 and 16

7. 14 and 10   8. 6 and 12   9. 8 and 12   10.   20 and 24

Helpful Hints

1	
2	
3	
4	
5	
6	
7	
8	
9	
10	
Score	

Problem Solving: A boy scored 153 points on a video game. This was 12 points more than his brother. How many points did his brother score?

89

Speed Drills

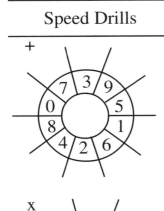

x

Review Exercises

1. Find all factors of 24.

2. Find the area.

12 ft.

5ft.

3. Classify this angle.

A
C
B

4. Circumference =

4 ft.

A multiple of a number is the product of that number and any whole number.

The multiples of a number can be found by multiplying it by 0, 1, 2, 3, 4, and so on.

Example: Find the first six multiples of 3.

3:   0,   3,   6,   9,   12,   15

These are found by multiplying 3 by 0, 1, 2, 3, 4, and 5

1	
2	
3	
4	
5	
6	
7	
8	
9	
10	
Score	

Complete the lists of multiples for each number.

S.   2: 0, 2, ☐,☐,☐,☐   S.   6: ☐, 6, ☐,☐, 24, ☐

1.   5: 0, 5, ☐,☐,☐,☐   2.   3: ☐, 3, ☐, 9, ☐,☐

3. 10: ☐, 10, 20, ☐,☐,☐   4.   4: ☐,☐,☐, 12, 16, 20

5. 11: 0, 11, ☐, 33, ☐, 55   6.   8: 0, 8, 16, ☐,☐,☐

7. 20: 0, 20, 40, ☐,☐,☐   8.   7: 0, 7, ☐, 21, ☐,☐

9. 30: 0, 30, 60, ☐,☐,☐   10. 9: 0, 9, 18, ☐, 36, ☐

90   The Smith family planned a 20 mile hike. The first day they hiked 7 miles, and the second day 5 miles. How many miles are left to hike?

Problem
Solving

Review Exercises	Speed Drills

1. List all factors of 12.

2. 2 is what % of 5?

3. Find the area:

4 ft.

8 ft.

4. List the first five multiples of 3.

Speed Drills

+

7	3	9
0		5
8		1
4	2	6

x

7	3	9
0		5
8		1
4	2	6

The least common multiples of two whole numbers is the smallest whole number, other than 0, that they both divide into evenly.

Examples: The least common multiple of:
2 and 3 is 6;   4 and 6 is 12;   3 and 9 is 9

Helpful Hints

Find the least common multiple of each pair of numbers.

			Hints
S. 3 and 4	S. 6 and 8	1. 3 and 5	1
			2
			3
2. 4 and 10	3. 5 and 6	4. 4 and 12	4
			5
			6
5. 2 and 6	6. 6 and 9	7. 5 and 10	7
			8
8. 7 and 5	9. 2 and 8	10. 15 and 10	9
			10
			Score

Problem Solving	A girl bought a bag of chips for $.34, a soda for $.25, and a candy bar for $.20. How much did she spend altogether?

91

Speed Drills

+

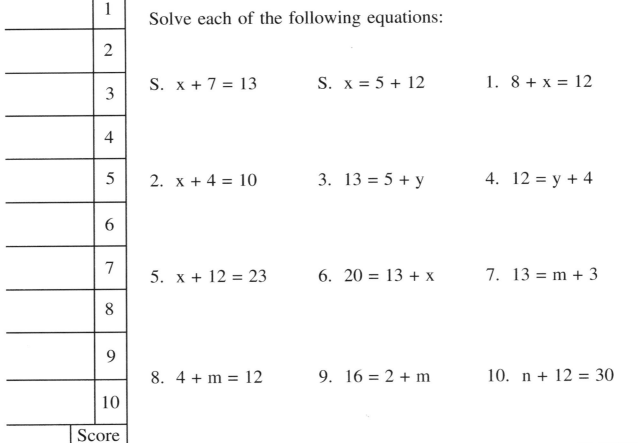

x

Helpful
Hints

Review Exercises

1.   3.6
      5.0
    + 3.2

2.   3.72
    - 1.45

3.   2.4
    x   3

4.   2) .46

A number sentence that has an equal sign, =, is called an equation. An equation may contain a variable, which is a letter used to represent an unspecified number. When you replace the variable with a number which makes the equation true, you have solved the equation.
Examples: Solve the following equations:

$x + 2 = 7$ $15 + x = 23$ $y + 10 = 20$
$5 + 2 = 7$ $15 + 7 = 23$ $10 + 20 = 20$
so $x = 5$ so $x = 7$ so $y = 10$

	1
	2
	3
	4
	5
	6
	7
	8
	9
	10
	Score

Solve each of the following equations:

S. $x + 7 = 13$ S. $x = 5 + 12$ 1. $8 + x = 12$

2. $x + 4 = 10$ 3. $13 = 5 + y$ 4. $12 = y + 4$

5. $x + 12 = 23$ 6. $20 = 13 + x$ 7. $13 = m + 3$

8. $4 + m = 12$ 9. $16 = 2 + m$ 10. $n + 12 = 30$

92

A playing field is in the shape of a square. If each side is 80 feet long, how many feet is it around the playing field?

Problem
Solving

Review Exercises	Speed Drills

1. Find the least common multiple of 4 and 6.

2. Find the greatest common factor of 20 and 15.

3. $2\overline{)\,.33}$

4. $\begin{array}{r} .3 \\ .4 \\ +\ .4 \\ \hline \end{array}$

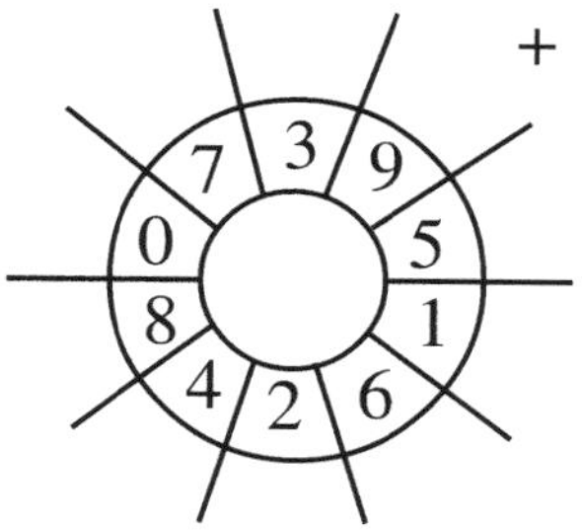

x

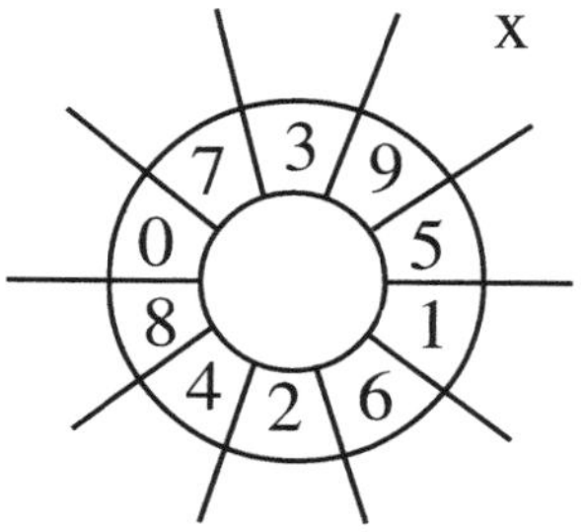

Remember, when you replace the variable in an equation with the number which makes the equation true, you have solved the equation.

Equations may contain addition, subtraction, multiplication or division.

Helpful
Hints

Solve each of the following equations:

S. $x - 2 = 5$ S. $6 = 12 - n$ 1. $n - 2 = 5$

2. $n - 5 = 4$ 3. $6 - x = 2$ 4. $2 = 5 - n$

5. $10 = n - 4$ 6. $8 - 3 = n$ 7. $9 - x = 3$

8. $20 - n = 15$ 9. $n - 7 = 18$ 10. $x - 3 = 11$

1	
2	
3	
4	
5	
6	
7	
8	
9	
10	
Score	

Problem Solving	A spelling test had 20 words. If Tran got 80% of the words correct, how many words did she get correct?

93

Speed Drills	Review Exercises

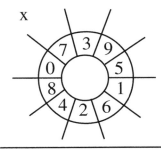

Helpful Hints

1. $\dfrac{2}{5} \div \dfrac{1}{4}$ 2. $\dfrac{2}{5} \times \dfrac{1}{3}$

3. $\dfrac{5}{8}$
$-\dfrac{1}{8}$

4. $\dfrac{3}{8}$
$-\dfrac{2}{8}$

When a number is written right beside a variable this means to multiply. The variable should be on the left.

$3n = 15$ $5n = 20$
means   means
$3 \times n = 15$ $5 \times n = 20$
$n = 5$ $n = 4$

1	
2	
3	
4	
5	
6	
7	
8	
9	
10	
Score	

Solve each of the following equations:

S. $2n = 12$ S. $3n = 24$ 1. $5n = 25$

2. $2n = 24$ 3. $12 = 3n$ 4. $28 = 4n$

5. $4n = 32$ 6. $5n = 35$ 7. $36 = 4n$

8. $7n = 35$ 9. $20 = 2n$ 10. $3n = 33$

A girl bought $3.24 worth of groceries. If she paid with a $5.00 bill, how much change should she receive? | **Problem Solving**

Review Exercises	Speed Drills

1. Classify this angle.

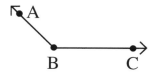

2. $6 \overline{)127}$

3. $\begin{array}{r} 35 \\ \times\ 23 \\ \hline \end{array}$

4. $234 + 14 + 123 =$

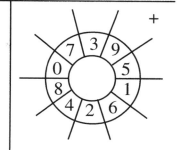

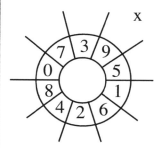

Equations with division may be written in two ways.
Examples:

$$x \div 2 = 5$$
$$10 \div 2 = 5$$
$$x = 5$$

$$\frac{n}{2} = 3$$

This means $n \div 2 = 3$
$$6 \div 2 = 3$$
$$n = 6$$

Helpful Hints

Solve each of the following equations:

S. $\dfrac{x}{3} = 4$ S. $x \div 2 = 4$ 1. $x \div 3 = 5$

2. $n \div 4 = 3$ 3. $\dfrac{n}{2} = 4$ 4. $\dfrac{12}{n} = 4$

5. $\dfrac{12}{2} = n$ 6. $\dfrac{n}{7} = 3$ 7. $\dfrac{n}{2} = 10$

8. $\dfrac{15}{x} = 3$ 9. $\dfrac{n}{3} = 7$ 10. $\dfrac{n}{4} = 6$

1	
2	
3	
4	
5	
6	
7	
8	
9	
10	
Score	

Problem Solving | An hour is 60 minutes. If a television program is $1\frac{1}{2}$ hours long, how many minutes long is the program?

95

Speed Drills	Review Exercises

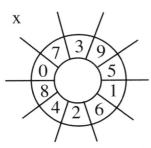

1. Find the perimeter.

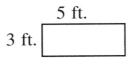

5 ft.

3 ft. [ ]

2. Find the area.

6 ft.

4 ft. [ ]

3. Find the circumference.

3 ft.

4. List all the factors of 20.

Helpful Hints	Use what you have learned to solve each of the following equations.

Solve each of the following equations:

1
2
3
4
5
6
7
8
9
10
Score

S. $\dfrac{x}{3} = 2$ S. $12 - n = 3$ 1. $x + 2 = 7$

2. $n - 7 = 2$ 3. $4n = 12$ 4. $n \div 2 = 5$

5. $13 = n + 10$ 6. $5 - n = 3$ 7. $18 = 3n$

8. $\dfrac{n}{2} = 7$ 9. $12 \div n = 6$ 10. $5 = 6 - n$

If hamburgers are $.72 each, how much would six of them cost? | Problem Solving

Find all factors of each number.

1.   20   2.   24   3.   30

Find the greatest common factor of each pair of numbers.

4.   16 and 10   5.   8 and 12   6.   12 and 15

Complete the list of multiples of each number.

7.   2: 0, 2, 4, □, □, □

8.   5: 0, □, 10, □, □, □

9.   7: □, □, □, □, □, 35

Find the least common multiple of each of the
pair of numbers.

10.   3 and 4   11.   4 and 6   12.   3 and 9

Solve each of the following equations.

13. $x + 2 = 5$ 14. $n - 2 = 5$ 15. $3n = 12$

16. $\dfrac{x}{2} = 4$ 17. $6 = n + 4$ 18. $7 - n = 3$

19. $n \div 5 = 2$ 20. $2n = 8$

1	
2	
3	
4	
5	
6	
7	
8	
9	
10	
11	
12	
13	
14	
15	
16	
17	
18	
19	
20	

Speed Drills

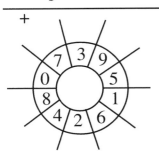

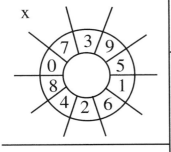

Helpful Hints

Review Exercises

1. Find the perimeter.

9 ft.
4 ft.
8 ft.

2. $\frac{1}{2}$ x $1\frac{1}{3}$ =

3. $\frac{1}{4}$
     $+ \frac{1}{3}$

4. $\frac{4}{5}$
     $- \frac{1}{2}$

←—|—|—|—|—|—|—|—|—|→
-4 -3 -2 0 1 2 3 4 5

Integers to the left of zero are negative and less than zero. Integers to the right of zero are positive and greater than zero. When two integers are on a number line, the one farthest to the right is greater. Think of positive integers as money you have. Think of negative integers as money you owe.

Example: -3 + -4 = -7   -3 + 5 = 2   3 + -7 = -4
           You owe 3 and   You have 5.   You have 3.
           you owe 4. So,   You owe 3.   You owe 7.
           you owe 7.   So, you have 2   So, you owe 4.

1	
2	
3	
4	
5	
6	
7	
8	
9	
10	
Score	

Solve each of the following:

S. -2 + -3 =   S. -6 + 2 =   1. 5 + -4 =

2. -5 + 4 =   3. -5 + -4 =   4. 9 + -2 =

5. -7 + 2 =   6. -6 + -5 =   7. -7 + -4 =

8. -3 + 9 =   9. 4 + -6 =   10. 12 + -15 =

600 people attended a concert. 40% of the people had reserved seats. How many had reserved seats?

Problem Solving

Review Exercises	Speed Drills

1. Write 2 to 5 in two
   other forms.

2. $\dfrac{3}{n} = \dfrac{6}{?}$

+

3. $3\overline{)\,.132}$

4. $\begin{array}{r} 6.2 \\ \times\;\; 3 \\ \hline \end{array}$

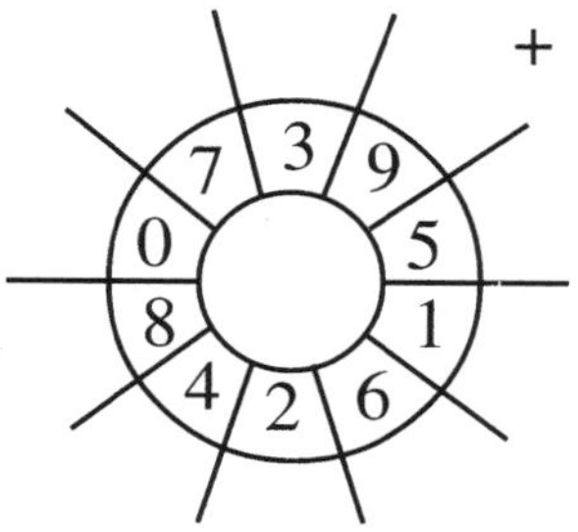

x

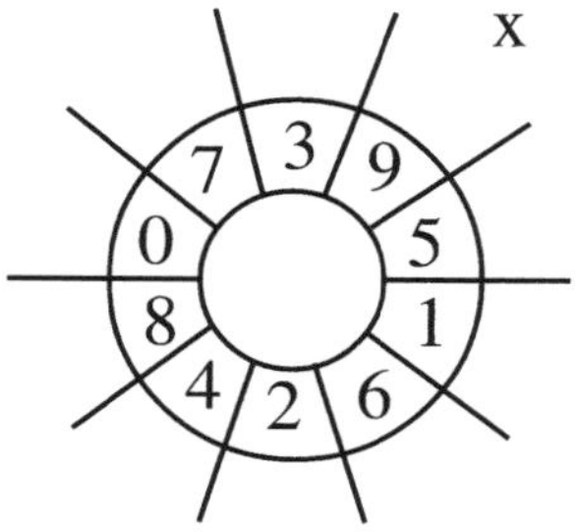

Use what you have learned to solve the following problems.

Think of positive integers as money you <u>have</u>.

Think of negative integers as money you <u>owe</u>.

Helpful
Hints

Solve each of the following.

S. -8 + 7 =   S. 8 + -7 =   1. -8 + -7 =

2. -15 + 13 =   3. 16 + -8 =   4. -7 + -5 =

5. -6 + -10 =   6. -7 + 12 =   7. 15 + -5 =

8. -6 + -8 =   9. -20 + 18 =   10. -25 + 27 =

1	
2	
3	
4	
5	
6	
7	
8	
9	
10	
Score	

Problem Solving	A team played 15 games and lost 3 of them. What percent did they lose?

99

Speed Drills

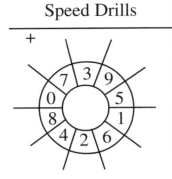

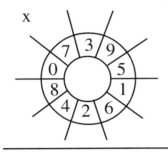

Helpful Hints

Review Exercises

1. Find the perimeter of a square with sides 8 feet.

2.   -6 + 8 =

3.   -7 + 5 =

4.   Solve the equation.
     n + 8 = 10

To subtract integers means to add to its opposite.
Examples:

* a double negative sign - - is the same as +
- - 7 = 7

2 - 5	-2 - 3	6 - -7
means	means	means
2 + -5 = -3	-2 + -3 = -5	6 + 7 = 13

	1
	2
	3
	4
	5
	6
	7
	8
	9
	10
	Score

Solve each of the following.

S. -5 - 2 =   S. 3 - -2 =   1. 2 - 7 =

2. 7 - 8 =   3. -3 - 5 =   4. 3 - -2 =

5. 4 - 6 =   6. -3 - 4 =   7. -3 - -4 =

8. -8 - 5 =   9. 3 - 8 =   10. 2 - -5 =

100

A business needs 120 postcards to mail to customers. If postcards come in boxes of 20, how many boxes does the business need?

Problem Solving

Review Exercises	Speed Drills

Review Exercises

1.   -2 - 3 =

2.   2 - 5 =

3.   -3 - -4 =

4.   2 + -7 =

Speed Drills

+

7 3 9
0   5
8   1
4 2 6

x

7 3 9
0   5
8   1
4 2 6

Use what you have learned to solve the following problems.

Think of positive integers as money you <u>have</u>.
Think of negative integers as money you <u>owe</u>.

Subtraction means to add it opposite. - -   means +
Examples:
    2 - 3 means
    2 + -3   7 - -2 = 7 + 2

Helpful Hints

Solve each of the following.

S. -8 + 6 =   S. 3 - 7 =   1. -7 + -2 =

2. 6 + -4 =   3. -7 - 3 =   4. 3 - -6 =

5. 6 + -10 =   6. -6 + -10 =   7. -6 + 10 =

8. 3 - 4 =   9. -3 - 4 =   10. -3 - -4 =

	Helpful Hints
1	
2	
3	
4	
5	
6	
7	
8	
9	
10	
Score	

Problem Solving   If eggs cost $1.13 per dozen, how much will 6 dozen cost?

101

Speed Drills	Review Exercises

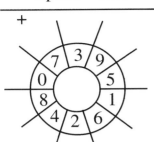

+

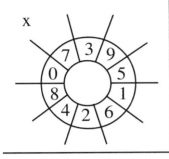

x

1. $2 \ x \ \dfrac{3}{4} =$ 2. $2\dfrac{1}{2} \div \dfrac{1}{2} =$

3. $\dfrac{1}{3} \ x \ 4 =$ 4. $\dfrac{2}{5} \div \dfrac{1}{10} =$

The product of two integers with the same sign is positive.

Example: -4 x -3 = 12

The product of two integers with different signs is negative.

Example: 3 x -2 = -6

	1	
	2	Solve each of the following.
	3	
	4	S. -2 x -6 = S. -5 x 3 = 1. 3 x -7 =
	5	
	6	2. -5 x 7 = 3. -5 x -8 = 4. -4 x -11 =
	7	
	8	5. -6 x 6 = 6. 7 x -4 = 7. -3 x -8 =
	9	
	10	8. -13 x -3 = 9. -11 x 7 = 10. 102 x -3 =
	Score	

Helpful
Hints

102

If the temperature at midnight was 12° and by 6 A.M. the temperature dropped another 15°. What was the temperature at 6 A.M.?

Problem
Solving

Review Exercises	Speed Drills

1.   5) 106   2.   -3 x -4 =

3.   7 + -6 =   4.   -3 – 7 =

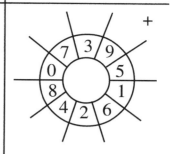

The quotient of two integers with the same sign is positive.

Example: $\frac{-12}{-2} = 6$

The quotient of two integers with different signs is negative.

Example: $12 \div -3 = -4$

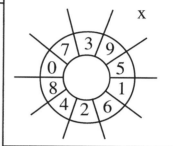

Helpful Hints

Solve each of the following:

S. $-8 \div 2 =$ S. $\frac{-10}{-5} =$ 1. $-6 \div -3 =$

2. $-15 \div 3 =$ 3. $18 \div -2 =$ 4. $\frac{-20}{-4} =$

5. $\frac{24}{-3} =$ 6. $-36 \div -4 =$ 7. $16 \div -2 =$

8. $-15 \div -5 =$ 9. $35 \div -5 =$ 10. $-18 \div 6 =$

1	
2	
3	
4	
5	
6	
7	
8	
9	
10	
Score	

Problem Solving	A girl earned 75 dollars a week for 5 weeks. How much money did she earn altogether?

103

	1
	2
	3
	4
	5
	6
	7
	8
	9
	10
	11
	12
	13
	14
	15
	16
	17
	18
	19
	20

1. $-7 + 6 =$ 2. $7 + -6 =$

3. $-7 + -6 =$ 4. $-9 + -6 =$

5. $8 + -2 =$ 6. $-7 + -2 =$

7. $2 - 6 =$ 8. $2 - -7 =$

9. $-3 - 5 =$ 10. $-5 - -4 =$

11. $8 - 3 =$ 12. $3 - 4 =$

13. $2 \times -6 =$ 14. $-3 \times -5 =$

15. $-5 \times 7 =$ 16. $8 \div -2 =$

17. $-14 \div -2 =$ 18. $-24 \div 3 =$

19. $\dfrac{24}{-2} =$ 20. $\dfrac{-15}{-5} =$

Review Exercises	Speed Drills

1. Find the circumference.

4 ft.

2. Find 12% of 30.

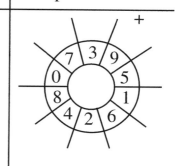

3. $\dfrac{2}{3}$ x $1\dfrac{1}{2}$ =

4. $2\dfrac{1}{2} \div 2$ =

Bar graphs are used to compare information

1. Read the title.
2. Understand the meaning of the numbers. Estimate if necessary.
3. Study the data.
4. Answer the questions, showing work if necessary.

Helpful Hints

Us the information in the graph to answer the questions.

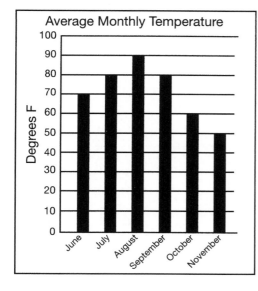

Average Monthly Temperature

S. Which month had the highest average temperature?

S. What was the average temperature in September?

1. In which month was the average temperature 50°?

2. Which months had the second highest average temperature?

3. Which month had the lowest average temperature?

4. What was the average temperature for July?

5. Which month had the second lowest temperature?

6. How many degrees higher was the average temperature in July than June?

7. How many degrees cooler was the average temperature in October than in September?

8. How many months had higher temperatures than June?

9. How many months had average temperatures lower than July?

10. Which two months had the same average temperature?

1	
2	
3	
4	
5	
6	
7	
8	
9	
10	
Score	

Problem Solving Bill worked 5 days and earned a total of 30 dollars. If he earned the same amount each day, how much did he earn each day?

105

Speed Drills	Review Exercises

+

1. Change $\frac{2}{5}$ to a decimal.

2. Change $\frac{3}{5}$ to a percent.

3. Change .3 to a percent.

4. Change .04 to a percent.

x

Helpful Hints

1. Read the title.
2. Understand the meaning of the numbers.
   Estimate if necessary.
3. Study the data.
4. Answer the questions, showing work if necessary.

1	Use the information in the graph to answer the questions.
2	
3	
4	
5	
6	
7	
8	
9	
10	

S. Which two cities had the same population?

S. What is the population of Springdale?

1. Which city has the highest population?

2. What is the population of Sun City?

3. What is the total population of Sun City and Winston?

4. How many more people live in Springdale than Lincoln?

5. Which city has the second lowest population?

6. Which city has twice as many people as Lincoln?

Populations of Cities in Riverdale County

Number of people in 100's

7. How many cities have a population greater than 500?
8. What is the total population of the two largest cities?
9. What is the population of Winston?
10. How many people must move to Lincoln to increase the population to 500?

Score

In an election Julie received 665 votes. John received 530. How many more votes did Julie receive than John?

Problem Solving

Review Exercises

1. Change $\frac{1}{4}$ to a percent.

2. Change .7 to a percent.

3. Find the area.

6 ft.

8 ft.

4. -7 + 9 =

+

x

Line graphs are used to show change.

1. Read the title.
2. Understand the meaning of the numbers. Estimate if necessary.
3. Study the data.
4. Answer the questions, showing work if necessary.

Helpful Hints

Use the information in the graph to answer the questions.

John's Math Test Scores

Percent Correct

100
95
90
85
80
75
70
65
60

Test 1 Test 2 Test 3 Test 4 Test 5 Test 6 Test 7

S. What was John's score on Test 5?
S. What were John's two lowest scores?
1. On which test did John score the lowest?
2. How many score did John have that were less than 95?
3. What is the difference between his highest and lowest scores?
4. How much higher was Test 6 than Test 5?
5. How many scores did John have that were higher than 90?
6. How much higher was Test 2 than Test 1?
7. On how many tests did John have a score of 95?
8. Does John seem to be improving in math?
9. How many scores did John have that were lower than 85?
10. What was John's score on Test 3?

1	
2	
3	
4	
5	
6	
7	
8	
9	
10	
Score	

Problem Solving A school has three fourth-grade classes, which each have 34 students. How many fourth-graders are there in the school?

107

Speed Drills

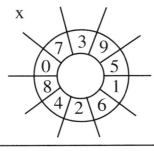

Helpful Hints

Review Exercises

1. $\dfrac{2}{5}$ + $\dfrac{4}{5}$

2. $\dfrac{7}{8}$ $- \dfrac{5}{8}$

3. 7 $- 2\dfrac{3}{5}$

4. $4\dfrac{1}{3}$ $- 2\dfrac{2}{3}$

1. Read the title.
2. Understand the meaning of the numbers.
   Estimate if necessary.
3. Study the data.
4. Answer the questions, showing
   work if necessary.

	1
	2
	3
	4
	5
	6
	7
	8
	9
	10
	Score

Use the information in the graph to answer the questions.

Johnson Music Shop CD Sales

(Line graph with y-axis 0 to 700 in increments of 100; x-axis months April, May, June, July, Aug., Sept. Points: April 300, May 200, June 400, July 500, Aug. 400, Sept. 700)

S. In which month were the most CD's sold?
S. How many CD's were sold in August?
1. Which month had the lowest total sales of CD's?
2. Which two months had the highest sales?
3. How many more CD's were sold in July than in August?
4. Which months had the same total sales?
5. Between which two months was the increase in sales the greatest?
6. What was the total number of CD's sold in the months of May and June?
7. How many more sales were there in September than August?
8. Which month had 300 more CD sales than May?
9. What is the difference in sales between the month with the most sales and the month with the least sales?
10. Does the store's sales seem to be increasing or decreasing?

Mary's test scores were 70, 90, and 80. What was her average score?

Problem Solving

Review Exercises	Speed Drills

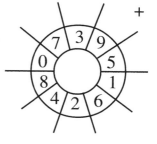

1. 12 + -18 =

2. 3 - -6 =

3. 4 x -6 =

4. Find 6% of 125.

A circle graph shows the relationship between the parts to the whole and to each other.

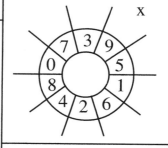

1. Read the title.
2. Understand the meaning of the numbers.
   Estimate if necessary.
3. Study the data.
4. Answer the questions, showing work if necessary.

Helpful
Hints

Use the information in the graph to answer the questions.

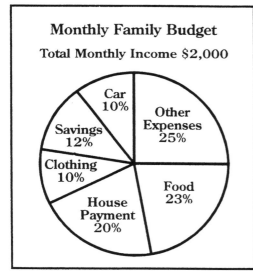

Monthly Family Budget

Total Monthly Income $2,000

Car 10%
Other Expenses 25%
Savings 12%
Clothing 10%
House Payment 20%
Food 23%

S. What percent of the family budget is used for food?

S. Which part of the budget requires the most expense?

1. What percent of the budget is used to pay for food and clothing?

2. After the car payment and house payment are paid, what percent of the budget is left?

3. Which two items require the same part of the budget?

4. What part of the budget would pay for medical expenses?

5. How many dollars are spent on the house payment? (Hint: Find 20% of $2,000.00)

6. What percent of the budget is for food and savings?

7. What is the family's total income for the month?

8. Which are the two most important items of the budget?

9. What is the least important item of the budget?

10. What percent of the budget is required for cars, savings and clothing?

1	
2	
3	
4	
5	
6	
7	
8	
9	
10	
Score	

Problem Solving	A man can walk $4\frac{1}{2}$ miles in an hour. How far can he walk in 2 hours?

109

Speed Drills

+

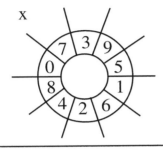

x

Helpful
Hints

Review Exercises

1. Reduce $\frac{15}{20}$ to its lowest terms.

2. Change $\frac{1}{5}$ to a percent.

3. 2 is what % of 8?

4. -24 ÷ -6 =

1. Read the title.
2. Understand the meaning of the numbers.
   Estimate if necessary.
3. Study the data.
4. Answer the questions, showing
   work if necessary.

	1
	2
	3
	4
	5
	6
	7
	8
	9
	10
	Score

Use the information in the graph to answer the questions.

Jane's School Day

- Sleep 9 hrs.
- Home Work 2 hrs.
- Chores 1 hr.
- Play 4 hrs.
- School 6 hrs.
- Meals 2 hrs.

S.   How many hours per day does Jane play?

S.   How much time does Jane spend each day at school and doing homework?

1.   If Jane starts her homework at 7:00 P.M., what time would she be finished?

2.   How many more hours does Jane sleep per day than play?

3.   How many hours does Jane spend at school per week?

4.   If Jane goes to bed at 9:00 P.M., what time does she get up in the morning?

5.   If school starts at 9:00 A.M., what time is school dismissed?

6.   How many hours does Jane spend in school in 4 days?

7.   How many hours does Jane spend on homework in 3 days?

8.   Which three activities take up the most of her time?

9.   How many more hours does Jane spend playing than doing homework each day?

10. If Jane's grades in school begin to drop, what could she do with her daily schedule to help bring them up?

110

A bedroom is in the shape of a rectangle with length 14 feet, and width 12 feet. What is the area of the bedroom?

Problem Solving

Review Exercises	Speed Drills

1.   385 + 226 + 43 =   2.   624
                                          x 53

3.   500   4.   5) 139
      - 236

+

x

Picture graphs are another way to compare statistics.

1. Read the title.
2. Understand the meaning of the numbers. Estimate if necessary.
3. Study the data.
4. Answer the questions, showing work if necessary.

Helpful Hints

Use the information in the graph to answer the questions.

Bikes Made By Street Bike Company

1986 🚲🚲
1987 🚲🚲🚲🚲
1988 🚲🚲🚲
1989 🚲🚲🚲🚲🚲🚲🚲
1990 🚲🚲🚲🚲🚲
1991 🚲🚲🚲🚲🚲🚲🚲🚲

Each 🚲 represents 1,000 bikes

S. How many bikes were made in 1990?
S. How many more bikes were made in 1987 than in 1986?
1. Which year produced two times as many bikes as 1988?
2. What is the total number of bikes produced in 1986, 1987, and 1988?
3. Which two years did the company make the most bikes?
4. Which two years did the company make the fewest bikes?
5. In 1987, half the bikes made were ladies' style. How many ladies' bikes were made in 1987?
6. What is the difference in bikes produced in 1991 and 1988?
7. What is the difference between the most productive and the least productive years?
8. If 1992 is expected to be double the production of 1990, how many bikes will be built in 1992?
9. What year produced half the number of bikes made in 1991?
10. 3,000 of the bikes made in 1989 were men's style bikes. How many were ladies' style bikes?

1	
2	
3	
4	
5	
6	
7	
8	
9	
10	
Score	

Problem Solving	Bill, John, and Mary together earned $414. If they wanted to share the money equally, how much would each one receive?	111

Speed Drills

+

x

Helpful Hints

Review Exercises

1. Find the circumference of a circle with a diameter of 6 feet.

2. Find the perimeter of a square with sides 13 feet?

3. Find the least common multiple of 5 and 3.

4. Find the greatest common factor of 15 and 20.

1. Read the title.
2. Understand the meaning of the numbers. Estimate if necessary.
3. Study the data.
4. Answer the questions, showing work if necessary.

	1
	2
	3
	4
	5
	6
	7
	8
	9
	10
	Score

Use the information in the graph to answer the questions.

America's Work Week

1950
1960
1970
1980
1990

Each symbol represents 10 hours

S. In which year was the work week the longest?

S. How much shorter was the work week in 1960 than in 1950?

1. How many hours long was the work week in 1980?

2. How many hours long was the work week in 1960?

3. How many hours did the work week increase between 1960 and 1970?

4. Which year's work week was 45 hours?

5. How many hours less was the work week in 1960 than in 1990?

6. Any work time over 40 hours is overtime. What was the average weekly overtime in 1970?

7. Which two years had the longest work weeks?

8. If an employee worked 50 weeks in 1950, how many hours did he work altogether that year?

9. How many hours did the work week decrease between 1970 and 1980?

10. If the work week in 1991 increased to 65 hours, how much overtime would there be each week?

112

A team played 12 games and won 9 of them. What percent of the games did the team win?

Problem Solving

Review Exercises	Speed Drills

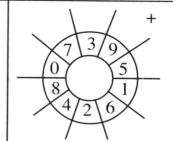

1. 3.7 + 5 + 2.16 =   2. 7.13 − 2.67 =

3. 6.5
    x 3.2

4. 2) 1.23

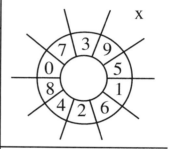

Numbers can be assigned to a point on a number line. Positive numbers are to the right of zero. Negative numbers are to the left of zero.

A   B   C

←++●+++++●+++++●+++++→
  -7 -6 -5 -4 -3 -2 -1 0 1 2 3 4 5 6 7 8 9

Helpful Hints

Examples: A is the graph of -5   A has a coordinate of -5
           B is the graph of -1   B has a coordinate of -1
           C is the graph of 5   C has a coordinate of 5

Use the number line to state the coordinates of the given points:

A D I N J P E T B S K R F L Q C M H G
←++++++++++++++++++++→
 -8 -7 -6 -5 -4 -3 -2 -1 0 1 2 3 4 5 6 7 8 9 10

1	
2	
3	
4	
5	
6	
7	
8	
9	
10	
Score	

S. B   S. D, E, and G   1. L and H

2. R and F   3. K, F, and C   4. N and A

5. G, H, I, and Q   6. H, D, and S

7. A, M, B, and P   8. B, C, and M

9. I, F, and P   10. L, P, H, and A

Problem Solving	A man bought 3 pens for $.35 each, and a notebook for $1.25. How much did he spend altogether?	113

Speed Drills	Review Exercises

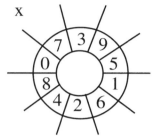

+

x

Helpful Hints

1. Find 6% of 70

2. 4 is what % of 5?

3. In a class of 40 students, 30% are boys. How many boys are in the class?

4. Sam took a test with 12 questions. If he got 9 correct, what % did he get correct?

Equations can be solved and graphed on a number line.

Examples:

			$\dfrac{m}{2} = 5$
x + 5 = 7	n − 3 = 2	3y = 21	
2 + 5 = 7	5 − 3 = 2	3 x 7 = 21	$\dfrac{10}{2} = 5$
x = 2	n = 5	y = 7	m = 10

	1
	2
	3
	4
	5
	6
	7
	8
	9
	10
	Score

Solve each equation and graph each solution on the number line. Also place each solution in the answer column.

S. x + 2 = 3   S. y − 2 = 5   1. c + 4 = 7

2. 5 − e = 0   3. 3d = 15   4. $\dfrac{f}{3} = 6$

5. n x 2 = 8   6. 3 + j = 14   7. 3 + k = 11

8. 4m = 28   9. 6 = n + 2   10. $\dfrac{r}{2} = 6$

If one pencil costs $.12, then how much would a dozen pencils cost?

Problem Solving

Review Exercises	Speed Drills

1.   -3 + 6 =   2.   -7 - 6 =

3.   3 x -6 =   4.   -32 ÷ -2 =

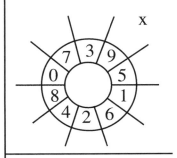

Ordered pairs can be graphed on a coordinate system.

The first number of an ordered pair shows how to move across.

The second number of an ordered pair shows how to move up and down.

Examples: To locate B, move across to the right to 3 and up 4. The ordered pair is (3,4).

To locate C, move across to the left to -6 and up 2. The ordered pair is (-5, 2).

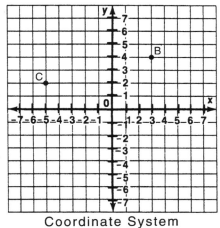

Coordinate System

Helpful Hints

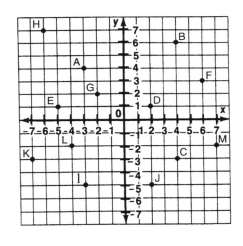

Use the coordinate system to find the ordered pair associated with each point.

S.   D   S.   L

1.   F   2.   J

3.   K   4.   E

5.   B   6.   C

7.   I   8.   G

9.   D   10.   H

1	
2	
3	
4	
5	
6	
7	
8	
9	
10	
Score	

Problem Solving	A coat was on sale for $32.25. If the regular price was $40.75, how much do you save buying the coat on sale?	115

Speed Drills	Review Exercises

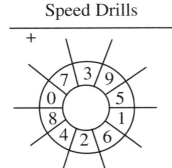

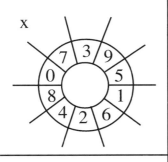

Helpful Hints

1.   235 + 16 + 325 =

2.   700 - 268 =

3.   543
     x 26

4.   3) 166

A point can be found by matching it with an ordered pair.

Examples: (-5, 3) is found by moving across to the left to -5, and up 3. This is represented by point B.

(6, 3) is found by moving across to the right to 6, and up 3. This is represented by point C.

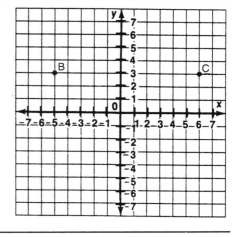

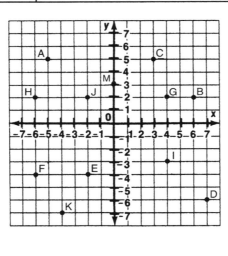

Use the coordinate system to find the point associated with each ordered pair.

S.   (6, 2)   S.   (-5, 5)

1.   (3, 5)   2.   (7, -6)

3.   (-6, -4)   4.   (0, 3)

5.   (-2, -4)   6.   (-2, 2)

7.   (-6, 2)   8.   (4, 2)

9.   (-4, -7)   10.   (4, -3)

1	
2	
3	
4	
5	
6	
7	
8	
9	
10	
Score	

116

If a man earns 25 dollars a day for 5 straight days, and earns 50 dollars on the sixth day, how much does he earn altogether?

Problem Solving

Reviewing Charts and Graphs

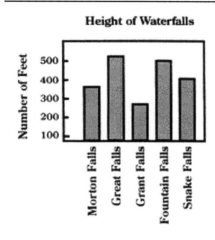

Height of Waterfalls

Number of Feet

Morton Falls, Great Falls, Grant Falls, Fountain Falls, Snake Falls

1. Which waterfall is the smallest?
2. Approximately how high is Great Falls?
3. Approximately how much higher is Morton Falls than Grant Falls?
4. Which waterfall is about the same height as Morton Falls?
5. Which waterfall is the fourth highest?

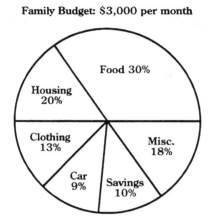

Family Budget: $3,000 per month

Food 30%, Housing 20%, Clothing 13%, Car 9%, Savings 10%, Misc. 18%

6. What percent of the family's money is spent on clothing?
7. What percent of the budget is spent on housing?
8. How many dollars are spent on housing per month? (Hint: Find 20% of $3,000)
9. What percent of the budget goes to savings?
10. What percent of the family budget is left after paying food, housing, and car expenses?

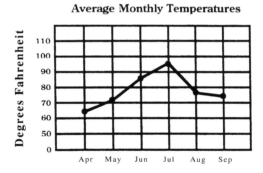

Average Monthly Temperatures

Degrees Fahrenheit

Apr May Jun Jul Aug Sep

11. What is the average temperature of May?
12. How much cooler was April than July?
13. Which was the second hottest month?
14. Which month's temperature dropped the most from the previous month?
15. What is the difference in temperature between the hottest month and the second hottest month?

Fish caught in Drakes Bay in 1991

Salmon
Perch
Cod
Bass
Snapper
Tuna

Each symbol represents 100 fish

16. How many perch were caught in 1991?
17. How many more snapper were caught than bass?
18. How many salmon and cod were caught?
19. If the average perch weighs 3 pounds, how many pounds were caught in 1991?
20. What are the three most commonly caught types of fish?

1	
2	
3	
4	
5	
6	
7	
8	
9	
10	
11	
12	
13	
14	
15	
16	
17	
18	
19	
20	

117

	1
	2
	3
	4
	5
	6
	7
	8
	9
	10
	11
	12
	13
	14
	15
	16
	17
	18
	19
	20

Use the number line to state the coordinates of the given points.

1. B   2. A, F, and G   3. G, L, and S   4. N, T, J, and H

Solve each equation and graph each solution on the number line. Be sure to label your answers. Also, place each solution in the answer column.

5. $n + 3 = 7$ 6. $x - 3 = 9$

7. $3y = 27$ 8. $\dfrac{m}{3} = 6$

Use the coordinate system to find the ordered pair associated with each point.

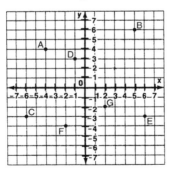

9.   A   10.   E   11.   B

12.   F   13.   C   14.   G

Use the coordinate system to find the point associated with each ordered pair.

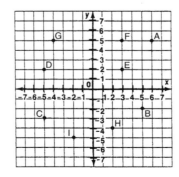

15.   (5, -2)   16.   (-4, 5)

17.   (2, -4)   18.   (-2, -5)

19.   (-5, -3)   20.   (3, 5)

118

Review Exercises	Speed Drills

1. $\dfrac{2}{3}$
$+\dfrac{1}{2}$

2. $\dfrac{7}{8}$
$-\dfrac{1}{2}$

3. $1\dfrac{1}{2} \times \dfrac{1}{3} =$

4. $1\dfrac{1}{4} \div \dfrac{1}{4} =$

Probability tells what chance, or how likely it is for an event to occur. Probability can be written as a fraction.

$$\text{Probability} = \frac{\text{number of ways a certain outcome can occur}}{\text{number of possible outcomes}}$$

Examples: If you toss a coin, what is the probability that it will show heads?
$\dfrac{1}{2}$ – heads is one outcome.
– there are two possible outcomes, heads or tails

There are 6 marbles in a jar. 3 are red, 2 are blue, and 1 is green. What is the probability that you will draw a blue one without looking?
$\dfrac{2}{6}$ – blue marbles
– marbles in the jar

Use the information below to answer the following questions.

There are 3 red marbles, 6 blue marbles, 2 black marbles, and 1 green marble in a can. Find the probability for each of the following.

S.   A red marble.   S.   A blue or green marble.

1.   A black marble.   2.   A green marble.

3.   A blue or red marble.   4.   Not a black marble.

5.   Not a red marble.   6.   Not a green or blue marble.

7.   A green, red, or blue marble.

8.   Not a blue marble.

9.   A green, red, or black marble.

10.   Not a blue or black marble.

Speed Drills

+

x

Helpful Hints

1	
2	
3	
4	
5	
6	
7	
8	
9	
10	
Score	

Problem Solving | Adult movie tickets are $3.50, and child tickets are $1.25. What would it cost for two adult tickets and two child tickets?

119

Speed Drills

+

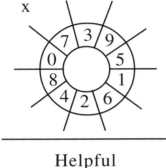

x

Helpful Hints

	1
	2
	3
	4
	5
	6
	7
	8
	9
	10
	Score

Review Exercises

1.   46.3 + 5 + 2.6 =   2.   7.2 - 3.67 =

3. $3.54   4.   3) 6.15
      x   7

Use what you have learned to answer the following questions.

Using the spinner to find the probability for each of the following. Find the probability of spinning once and landing on each of the following.

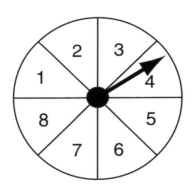

S. a three   S. an even number

1. a seven   2. not a five

3. an odd number

4. a number less than five   5.   a number greater than 6

6. a nine   7. a one or an eight   8.   an even number or a 5

9. a number greater than 3   10.   a number which is a factor of 6

Mary has 6 dollars. Susan has three times as much money as Mary. How much money do the two girls have altogether?

| Problem Solving |

Review Exercises	Speed Drills

1. Change .3
    to a percent

2. Change .03
    to a percent.

3. Change $\frac{4}{5}$
    to a percent

4. Find 5% of 65.

Statistics involves gathering and recording data. Number facts about events or objects are called data. The range is the difference between the greatest number and the least number in a list of data. The mode is the number which appears the most in a list of data.
Example: Find the range and mode for the list of data.
            12, 10, 1, 7, 4, 7, 5
            First, list numbers from least to greatest.
            1, 4, 5, 7, 7, 10, 12   The range is 12 - 1 = 11
            The mode is 7 which appears the most.

Helpful Hints

Arrange the data in order from least to greatest. Then find the range and mode.

S.   7, 4, 1, 8, 2, 5, 4

S.   6, 2, 7, 6, 8, 2, 5, 6, 3

1.   7, 4, 8, 2, 4, 7, 7

2.   25, 17, 30, 39, 16, 24, 30

3.   1, 3, 6, 3, 4, 6, 11, 9

4.   1, 6, 17, 8, 9, 20, 9

5.   7, 3, 1, 3, 1, 3, 8, 4

6.   3, 14, 8, 6, 11, 8, 14, 8

7.   1, 10, 2, 9, 3, 8, 2, 7

8.   85, 91, 90, 86, 91, 87

9.   1, 10, 2, 9, 2, 7, 2, 8

10.   20, 2, 19, 1, 2, 16, 3

1	
2	
3	
4	
5	
6	
7	
8	
9	
10	
Score	

Problem Solving   Bill has 12 dollars. Jose has half as much money as Bill. How much money do they have altogether?

121

Speed Drills	Review Exercises

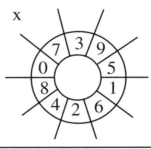

+

1. -7 + 12 =

2. -6 - 4 =

3. 3 x -8 =

4. -24 ÷ -3 =

x

The mean of a list of data is found by adding all the items in the list and then dividing by the number of items.

The median is the middle number, when the list of data is arranged from least to greatest.

Example: Find the mean and median for the list of data.
1, 2, 5, 6, 6

Helpful Hints

Median = 5   ↗   Mean = $\dfrac{1 + 2 + 5 + 6 + 6}{5} = \dfrac{20}{5} = 4$

	1
	2
	3
	4
	5
	6
	7
	8
	9
	10
	Score

Arrange the data in order from least to greatest. Then find the mean and median for each list of data.

S.   1, 5, 2, 4, 3

S.   6, 1, 7, 4, 2, 6, 2

1.   2, 7, 1, 4, 1

2.   1, 5, 7, 1, 2, 2, 3

3.   5, 25, 10, 20, 15

4.   1, 1, 1, 3, 3, 3, 4, 1, 1

5.   8, 5, 2, 9, 3, 6, 9

6.   126, 136, 110

7.   7, 3, 4, 2, 4

8.   3, 1, 4, 7, 5

9.   2, 10, 4, 8, 1

10.   50, 70, 30

If 3 cans of juice cost $1.14, what is the cost of 1 can?

Problem Solving

Review Exercises | Speed Drills

1. 6 ft. | 3 ft.

Perimeter =

2. 13 ft.

Area =

3. 3 ft.

Circumference =

4. 6 ft. / 5 ft.

Area =

Use what you have learned to answer the following questions. | Helpful Hints

Arrange the data in order from least to greatest than answer the questions.

2, 8, 6, 2, 7

S. What is the range? S. What is the mode?

1. What is the mean? 2. What is the median?

1, 9, 2, 7, 2, 3, 4

3. What is the median? 4. What is the mode?

5. What is the range? 6. What is the mean?

2, 11, 8, 6, 1, 2, 5

7. What is the range? 8. What is the mode?

9. What is the mean? 10. What is the median?

1	
2	
3	
4	
5	
6	
7	
8	
9	
10	
Score	

Problem Solving: Alex had test scores of 80, 70, and 90. What was his mean score?

123

_____	1
_____	2
_____	3
_____	4
_____	5
_____	6
_____	7
_____	8
_____	9
_____	10
_____	11
_____	12
_____	13
_____	14
_____	15
_____	16
_____	17
_____	18
_____	19
_____	20

There are 4 green marbles, 3 red marbles, 2 white marbles, and 1 blue marble in a can. What is the probability for each of the following?

1. a red marble   2. a green marble   3. a green or blue marble

4. not a red marble   5. a green, red or blue marble   6. not a green marble

Use the spinner to find the probability of spinning once and landing on each of the following.

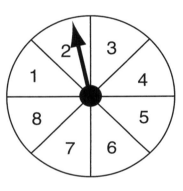

7. a five   8. an odd number

9. a number greater than three

10. a one or a three

11. a number less than five

12. a one or a six

Arrange the data in order from least to greatest, then answer the questions.

2, 5, 4, 10, 4

13.   What is the range?   14.   What is the mode?

15.   What is the mean?   16.   What is the median?

2, 5, 2, 1, 3, 7, 8

17.   What is the mode?   18.   What is the mean?

19.   What is the range?   20.   What is the median?

Review Exercises	Speed Drills

1. Express as a ratio.

⚪ ⚪
⬜ ⬜ ⬜

2. Solve the proportion.

$$\frac{2}{3} = \frac{6}{?}$$

3. Solve the equation.
   $13 - x = 4$

4. Solve the equation.
   $$\frac{x}{3} = 5$$

1. Read the problem carefully.
2. Find the important facts and numbers.
3. Decide what operations to use.
4. Solve the problem.

*Sometimes drawing a practice diagram can help.
* Sometimes a formula is necessary.
* Sometimes reading a problem more than once helps.
* Show your work.

Helpful Hints

S. There are 2 fourth grade classes with enrollment of 32 and 35. How many fourth graders are there in all?

S. A family drove 215 miles each day for 5 days. How far did they drive altogether?

1. The attendance at the Raider's game last year was 1,235. This year 1,783 attended. What was the increase in attendance?

2. 5 friends earned 735 dollars. If they want to divide the money evenly, how much will each person receive?

3. A school put on a play. Monday 265 attended, 136 attended Tuesday and 243 attended Wednesday. What was the total attendance?

4. John scored 1,234 points on a video game. Julie scored 1,455 points. How many more points did Julie receive than John?

5. If a car travels 65 miles per hour, how far does it travel in 8 hours?

6. A car traveled 240 miles in 4 hours. What was the average speed per hour?

7. A car's gas tank holds 8 gallons. If the car can travel 13 miles per gallon, how far can the car travel?

8. A banner is in the shape of a triangle with sides 14 feet, 15 feet, and 17 feet. How many feet is it around the banner?

9. A rope is 112 feet long. If it is cut into pieces 2 feet long, how many pieces will there be?

10. A library has 2,160 fiction books, 1,160 nonfiction books, and 253 reference books. How many books are there in all?

1	
2	
3	
4	
5	
6	
7	
8	
9	
10	
Score	

125

Speed Drills

$+$

7 3 9
0   5
8   1
4 2 6

x

7 3 9
0   5
8   1
4 2 6

1. $\begin{array}{r} \frac{3}{5} \\ + \frac{1}{2} \\ \hline \end{array}$

2. $\begin{array}{r} \frac{7}{8} \\ - \frac{1}{4} \\ \hline \end{array}$

3. $\frac{2}{3}$ of $\frac{3}{4}$ =

4. $\frac{1}{2}$ of $1\frac{1}{3}$ =

Helpful Hints

1. Read the problem carefully.
2. Find the important facts and numbers.
3. Decide what operations to use.
4. Solve the problem.

*Sometimes drawing a practice diagram can help.
* Sometimes a formula is necessary.
* Sometimes reading a problem more than once helps.
* Show your work.

1	
2	
3	
4	
5	
6	
7	
8	
9	
10	
Score	

S. A cook uses $2\frac{1}{5}$ cups of flour for a cake and $1\frac{1}{3}$ cups of flour for a pie. How much flour did he use?

S. A ribbon is $2\frac{1}{2}$ feet long. It was cut into pieces $\frac{1}{2}$ feet long. How many pieces were there?

1. Bill weighs $90\frac{1}{2}$ pounds. Sam weighs $93\frac{3}{4}$ pounds. How much more does Sam weigh than Bill?

2. Steve earned 15 dollars and spent $\frac{2}{3}$ of it. How much did he spend?

3. A book weighs $1\frac{1}{2}$ pounds. How many pounds do 3 books weigh?

4. A woman can drive to work in $7\frac{1}{2}$ minutes. She can drive home in $5\frac{1}{2}$ minutes. What is the total time she has to drive to and from work?

5. A flag is in the shape of a square. Each side is $3\frac{1}{2}$ feet long. What is the perimeter of the flag?

6. Natalie earned $5\frac{1}{2}$ dollars and spent $2\frac{1}{4}$ dollars. How much money did she have left?

7. A man worked $2\frac{1}{2}$ hours on Monday and $1\frac{1}{4}$ hours on Tuesday. How many hours did he work altogether?

8. Linda worked $3\frac{1}{2}$ hours on Monday and $1\frac{3}{5}$ hours on Tuesday. How many more hours did she work on Monday than on Tuesday?

9. A girl can jog 6 miles in an hour. At this pace how far can she jog in $2\frac{1}{2}$ hours?

10. A factory can make a tire in $1\frac{1}{2}$ minutes. How many tires can it make in 6 minutes?

126

Review Exercises	Speed Drills

1. $1.23 + $3.16 + $4.24 =

2. $7.00
     + $2.58

3. $2.17
   x   6

4.   6) 4.14

1. Read the problem carefully.
2. Find the important facts and numbers.
3. Decide what operations to use.
4. Solve the problem.

*Sometimes drawing a practice diagram can help.
* Sometimes a formula is necessary.
* Sometimes reading a problem more than once helps.
* Show your work.

Helpful Hints

S. If a dozen pencils cost $1.17, how much do 6 dozen cost?

S. A desk is shaped like a rectangle. If the length is 2.6 feet, and the width is 1.3 feet, what is the perimeter of the desk?

1. Beef costs $3.15 per pound. Fish costs $2.85 per pound. How much more is beef per pound.

2. A man bought a chair for $35.50, a desk for $125.55, and a lamp for $24.75. What was the total cost of the items?

3. 5 cans of pet food cost $7.25. What is the price per can?

4. A car travels 50.6 miles in one hour. At this rate, how far can it travel in 5 hours?

5. Steve can earn $7.25 per day. How much can he earn in 5 days?

6. A sack of potatoes costs $2.50. If there are 5 pounds of potatoes in a sack, what is the price per pound?

7. A bike was on sale for $125.50. If the regular price was $175.75, how much could he save buying it on sale?

8. Ellen weighs 85.2 pounds. Mary weighs 75.9 pounds. What is their combined weight?

9. If 3 pounds of butter cost $5.34, what is the price per pound?

10. A man bought a quart of milk for $1.23. If he paid with a $5.00 bill, how much change should he get?

1	
2	
3	
4	
5	
6	
7	
8	
9	
10	
Score	

127

Speed Drills

+

x

Review Exercises

1. $\dfrac{1}{2}$
   $+\ \dfrac{1}{3}$

2. $3.4 + 2.66 =$

3. $\dfrac{7}{8}$
   $-\ \dfrac{1}{2}$

4. $3.7 - 1.63 =$

Helpful Hints

1. Read the problem carefully.
2. Find the important facts and numbers.
3. Decide what operations to use.
4. Solve the problem.

*Sometimes drawing a practice diagram can help.
* Sometimes a formula is necessary.
* Sometimes reading a problem more than once helps.
* Show your work.

1	
2	
3	
4	
5	
6	
7	
8	
9	
10	
Score	

S. A rope 64 feet long is to be cut into pieces 4 feet long. How many pieces will there be?

S. If candy bars cost $.15 each, how much will 6 candy bars cost?

1. Tim had $3.25. If he spent $1.55, how much money does he have left?

2. 4 loaves of bread cost $4.24. How much does 1 loaf of bread cost?

3. Steve had a total score of 285 on 3 tests. What was his average score?

4. A boy can earn $1\frac{1}{2}$ dollars in 1 hour. How much can he earn in 4 hours?

5. A carpenter needs to glue together two boards with lengths of 3.8 inches and 7.6 inches. What would the length be after they are glued together?

6. A school has 600 students. If they are to be grouped into 20 equally sized classes, how many students will be in each class?

7. A rancher owns 40 cows. If he decides to sell $\frac{1}{5}$ of them, how many cows would he sell?

8. A farm is in the shape of a square. If each side is 7 miles, what is the perimeter of the farm?

9. A board was 7 feet long. If $2\frac{1}{2}$ feet were cut off, how much of the board was left?

10. Steak costs $2.70 per pound. How much will 5 pounds of steak cost?

128

Review Exercises	Speed Drills

1. $2 \overline{)46}$

2. $5 \overline{)116}$

3. $20 \overline{)433}$

4. $22 \overline{)462}$

+

x

1. Read the problem carefully.
2. Find the important facts and numbers.
3. Decide what operations to use.
4. Solve the problem.

*Sometimes drawing a practice diagram can help.
* Sometimes a formula is necessary.
* Sometimes reading a problem more than once helps.
* Show your work.

Helpful Hints

S. Stan's test scores were 20, 22, and 23. What was his average score?

S. A farmer has 7 boxes of seed which weigh 8 pounds each, and a sack of apples which weigh 12 pounds. What is the total weight of the seed and apples?

1. Last week a boy worked 6 hours per day for five days. This week he worked 20 hours. How many hours did he work in all?

2. An orchard has 12 rows of trees with 6 trees in each row. If each tree produces 5 bushels of fruit, how many bushels will be produced in all?

3. Buses hold 50 people. If 70 parents and 130 students, are attending a football game, how many buses will they need?

4. A school has 160 boys and 140 girls. If they are grouped into classes of 30 each, how many classes are there?

5. A family traveled 200 miles per day for 5 days and 260 miles on the sixth day. How many miles did they travel in all?

6. A tank holds 250 gallons of fuel. If 55 gallons were removed one day and 23 gallons the next, how many gallons are left?

7. Five buses hold 50 people each. If 165 people buy tickets for a trip, how many seats won't be taken?

8. Bill worked 7 hours on Monday, 5 hours on Tuesday, and 6 hours on Wednesday. If he earns $5.00 per hour, how much did he earn?

9. A man picked 5 baskets of fruit per day for seven days. He sold 19 baskets. How many baskets were left?

10. A family was taking a 400 mile trip. They drove 125 miles the first day and 65 miles the second. How many miles are left to travel?

1	
2	
3	
4	
5	
6	
7	
8	
9	
10	
Score	

129

Speed Drills	Review Exercises

+

1.   4.2 + 7.6 + 6.83 =

2.   24.6
      x   7

x

3.   5.3 – 2.78 =

4.   3) $6.30

Helpful Hints

1. Read the problem carefully.
2. Find the important facts and numbers.
3. Decide what operations to use.
4. Solve the problem.

*Sometimes drawing a practice diagram can help.
* Sometimes a formula is necessary.
* Sometimes reading a problem more than once helps.
* Show your work.

1	
2	
3	
4	
5	
6	
7	
8	
9	
10	
Score	

S. A man bought 3 bags of chips at $.49 each, and a pizza for $7.45. How much did he spend in all?

S. Jim bought a hammer for $3.25 and a bag of nails for $.55. If he paid with a $5.00 bill, how much change should he receive?

1. A girl worked 5 hours and was paid $2.50 per hour. If she bought a pen for $1.75, how much of her pay was left?

2. Cans of peas cost 2 for $.55. How much would 6 cans cost?

3. Jeans are on sale for $8.50. If the regular price is $9.75, how much would be saved buying 3 pairs of jeans on sale?

4. Three friends earned $2.50 on Monday, $3.00 on Tuesday, and $2.00 on Wednesday. If they divided the money evenly, how much would each receive?

5. A man bought 3 shirts for $9.00 each and a belt for $7.50. How much did he spend in all?

6. A yard is 10 feet long and 15 feet wide. If fencing cost $2.00 per foot, how much would it cost to build a fence around the yard?

7. 5 cans of tuna cost $2.50. Cans of beef cost $.79 each. How much would it cost for 1 can of tuna and 1 can of beef?

8. A man bought 2 hammers for $1.25 each and 3 saws for $2.50 each. What was the total cost?

9. Tom's times for the 100 yard dash were 11.8 seconds, 12.2 seconds, and 12.3 seconds. What was his average time?

10. A man bought 3 gallons of gas at $1.60 per gallon. If he paid with a $10.00 bill, what would be the change?

130

Reviewing Problem Solving

1. Johnson's school enrollment is 573 and Jefferson's school enrollment is 727. What is the total enrollment for both schools?

2. A man plans to drive 215 miles each day. How far will he drive in 3 days?

3. John needs $85.00 to buy a bike. He has already saved $58.00. How much more money is needed to buy the bike?

4. A can of juice costs $1.16. How much will it cost for 4 cans of juice?

5. A club earned $6.36. If the money is divided equally by 3 members, how much would each member get?

6. A shirt was on sale for $8.25. If the regular price was $9.75, how much is saved buying the shirt on sale?

7. Jessica's test scores were 21, 24, and 15. What was her average score?

8. 2 cans of corn cost $1.12. What is the price for 1 can of corn?

9. A boy bought 3 sodas for $.55 each, and a bag of chips for $1.15. How much did he spend in all?

10. There are 113 sixth graders at Monroe School, and 137 fifth graders. How many more fifth graders are there than sixth graders?

11. A man bought a pen for $1.15 and a ruler for $1.05. If he paid with a $5.00 bill, how much change should he receive?

12. A family set out on a 30 mile hike. The first day they hiked 8 miles, and the second day they hiked 6 miles. How many miles were left to complete the hike?

13. A theater has 7 rows of seats. There are 8 seats in each row. If 48 seats are taken, how many seats are empty?

14. Ann has 6 dollars. Bill has twice as much money as Ann. How much money do they have altogether?

15. Sue made 12 bracelets this week and 14 bracelets last week. If she sold half of the bracelets, how many bracelets did she sell?

16. Steve worked 5 hours Monday and 7 hours Tuesday. If he was paid 3 dollars per hour, how much did he earn?

17. A painter started with 6 cans of paint. If he has used 3 cans of paint, how many cans are left?

18. Buses hold 50 people. If 75 students and 75 parents plan to attend a game, how many buses will be needed?

19. Steak costs $1.25 per pound. How much does 4 pounds cost?

20. Laura weighs 96.3 pounds, and Maria weighs 86.4 pounds. What is their total weight?

1	
2	
3	
4	
5	
6	
7	
8	
9	
10	
11	
12	
13	
14	
15	
16	
17	
18	
19	
20	

131

Final Review – Whole Numbers

1
2
3
4
5
6
7
8
9
10
11
12
13
14
15
16
17
18
19
20

1. $\begin{array}{r} 34 \\ + 23 \\ \hline \end{array}$ 2. $\begin{array}{r} 356 \\ + 374 \\ \hline \end{array}$ 3. $\begin{array}{r} 26 \\ 23 \\ + 34 \\ \hline \end{array}$ 4. $\begin{array}{r} 346 \\ 27 \\ + 524 \\ \hline \end{array}$

5. $328 + 26 + 145 =$ 6. $\begin{array}{r} 7,243 \\ + 4,327 \\ \hline \end{array}$

7. $\begin{array}{r} 27 \\ - 15 \\ \hline \end{array}$ 8. $\begin{array}{r} 342 \\ - 125 \\ \hline \end{array}$ 9. $\begin{array}{r} 600 \\ - 76 \\ \hline \end{array}$

10. $\begin{array}{r} 713 \\ - 245 \\ \hline \end{array}$ 11. $\begin{array}{r} 3,542 \\ - 1,751 \\ \hline \end{array}$

12. $\begin{array}{r} 22 \\ \times \ \ 3 \\ \hline \end{array}$ 13. $\begin{array}{r} 27 \\ \times \ \ 4 \\ \hline \end{array}$ 14. $\begin{array}{r} 523 \\ \times \ \ 6 \\ \hline \end{array}$

15. $\begin{array}{r} 35 \\ \times \ 24 \\ \hline \end{array}$ 16. $\begin{array}{r} 365 \\ \times \ 34 \\ \hline \end{array}$ 17. $2\overline{)46}$

18. $4\overline{)526}$ 19. $4\overline{)1396}$ 20. $22\overline{)4664}$

132

Final Review – Fractions and Mixed Numerals

1. $\dfrac{1}{5}$
    $+ \dfrac{2}{5}$

2. $\dfrac{3}{7}$
    $+ \dfrac{5}{7}$

3. $\dfrac{2}{5}$
    $+ \dfrac{1}{2}$

4. $\dfrac{3}{5}$
    $+ \dfrac{1}{2}$

5. $3\dfrac{1}{3}$
    $+ 2\dfrac{1}{2}$

6. $\dfrac{3}{5}$
    $- \dfrac{1}{5}$

7. 5
    $- 2\dfrac{1}{3}$

8. $\dfrac{3}{4}$
    $- \dfrac{1}{2}$

9. $3\dfrac{2}{3}$
    $- 1\dfrac{1}{2}$

10. $5\dfrac{3}{5}$
    $- 1\dfrac{1}{2}$

11. $\dfrac{1}{2} \times \dfrac{1}{4} =$

12. $\dfrac{3}{4} \times \dfrac{5}{6} =$

13. $\dfrac{1}{3} \times 9 =$

14. $4 \times 1\dfrac{1}{2} =$

15. $\dfrac{1}{2} \times 5 =$

16. $1\dfrac{1}{2} \times 1\dfrac{1}{3} =$

17. $\dfrac{1}{3} \div \dfrac{1}{2} =$

18. $\dfrac{2}{3} \div \dfrac{1}{2} =$

19. $1\dfrac{1}{2} \div \dfrac{1}{2} =$

20. $2\dfrac{1}{2} \div \dfrac{1}{4} =$

1	
2	
3	
4	
5	
6	
7	
8	
9	
10	
11	
12	
13	
14	
15	
16	
17	
18	
19	
20	

133

Final Review – Decimal Operations

1
2
3
4
5
6
7
8
9
10
11
12
13
14
15
16
17
18
19
20

1.　3.2
　　+ 4.3

2.　3.12
　　5.00
　　+ 2.3

3.　4.3 + 3.14 + 2.6 =

4.　$213.62
　　+ $243.55

5.　3.16 + 2 + 4.16 =

6.　5.1
　　− 3.2

7.　3.2
　　− 1.14

8.　6.44
　　− 2.16

9.　5.1
　　− 2.36

10.　5 − 2.34 =

11.　2.1
　　x　5

12.　1.24
　　x　3

13.　.413
　　x　5

14.　.23
　　x　21

15.　2.14
　　x　13

16.　$3.16
　　x　7

17.　2) 4.6

18.　3) .123

19.　2) .23

20.　5) 5.75

134

Final Review – Ratio, Proportion, Percent

Write numbers 1 and 2 as a ratio expressed in fraction form.

1.   5 pennies to 2 dimes   2.   7 to 6

For numbers 3 and 4 solve each proportion.

3. $\dfrac{2}{3} = \dfrac{4}{?}$ 4. $\dfrac{3}{4} = \dfrac{6}{?}$

Change numbers 5 through 8 to a percent.

5. $\dfrac{17}{100} =$ 6. $\dfrac{3}{10} =$ 7. $.13 =$ 8. $.4 =$

Change numbers 9 through 11 to a decimal and a fraction.

9. $12\% = .\quad = \quad -$ 10. $3\% = .\quad = \quad -$

11. $20\% = .\quad = \quad -$

12.   Find 12% of 30.   13.   Find 3% of 60.

14.   2 is what % of 5?   15.   2 is what % of 8?

16.   Change $\dfrac{1}{5}$ to a percent.   17.   Change $\dfrac{1}{4}$ to a percent.

18.   A man earned 30 dollars. If he put 20% of it into the bank, how much did he put into the bank?

19.   A girl baked 8 cakes. If she sold 2 of them, what percent did she sell?

20.   Al took a test with 20 questions, a student got 80% correct. How many questions did he get correct?

1	
2	
3	
4	
5	
6	
7	
8	
9	
10	
11	
12	
13	
14	
15	
16	
17	
18	
19	
20	

135

Final Review – Geometry

Use this figure to answer questions 1-8

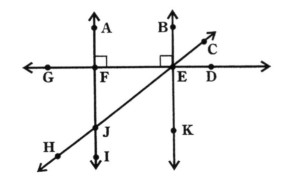

1. Name 2 parallel lines
2. Name 2 perpendicular lines
3. Name a line segment
4. Name a ray
5. Name an acute angle
6. Name an obtuse angle
7. Name a straight angle
8. Name a right angle

Triangle A

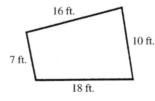

Triangle B

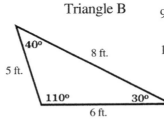

9. Classify Triangle A by its sides and angles
10. Classify Triangle B by its sides and angles

11. Find the perimeter

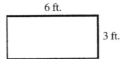

12. Find the Circumference

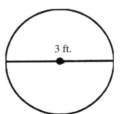

13. What is the length of the diameter?

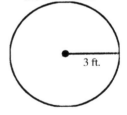

14. Find the area.

15. Find the area.

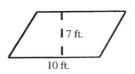

16. Find the area.

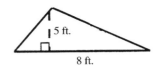

17. Find the area.

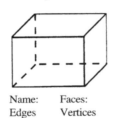

18. Identify and count the parts.

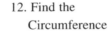

Name: _____ Faces: _____
Edges _____ Vertices _____

19. Find the perimeter.

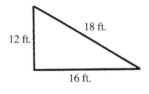

20. Find the perimeter of a square with sides of 16 ft.

136

Final Review – Number Theory and Algebra

Find all factors of each number.

1.   12   2.   15   3.   20

Find the greatest common factor of each pair of numbers.

4.   6 and 8   5.   8 and 12   6.   20 and 15

Complete the list of multiples of each number.

7.   2: 0, 2, 4, ☐, ☐, ☐

8.   3: 0, ☐, 6, ☐,☐, 15

9.   4: ☐,☐,☐,☐,☐ , 20

Find the least common multiples of each of the pair of numbers.

10.   3 and 2   11.   4 and 6   12.   4 and 8

Solve each of the following equations.

13.   x + 1 = 3   14.   x – 2 = 3   15.   3x = 15

16. $\frac{x}{2}$ = 4   17.   7 = x + 4   18.   5 – n = 2

19.   x ÷ 2 = 4   20.   3n = 12

1	
2	
3	
4	
5	
6	
7	
8	
9	
10	
11	
12	
13	
14	
15	
16	
17	
18	
19	
20	

137

Final Review – Integers

1
2
3
4
5
6
7
8
9
10
11
12
13
14
15
16
17
18
19
20

1. $5 + -3 =$

2. $-5 + 3 =$

3. $-5 + -3 =$

4. $-6 + -2 =$

5. $7 + -5 =$

6. $-3 + -5 =$

7. $2 - 6 =$

8. $2 - -5 =$

9. $-2 - 3 =$

10. $3 \times -5 =$

11. $-3 \times -6 =$

12. $-6 \times 4 =$

13. $-8 \times -4 =$

14. $3 \times -12 =$

15. $-6 \times -4 =$

16. $8 \div -2 =$

17. $-12 \div 3 =$

18. $-14 \div -2 =$

19. $\dfrac{-12}{2} =$

20. $\dfrac{-9}{-3} =$

138

Final Review – Charts and Graphs

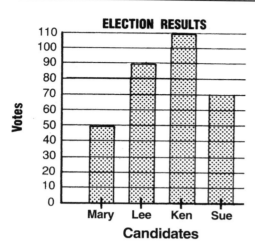

ELECTION RESULTS

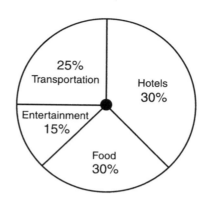

Transportation 25%
Hotels 30%
Entertainment 15%
Food 30%

1. Which candidate got the most votes?
2. How many votes did Sue receive?
3. How many more votes did Lee get than Mary?
4. Together, how many votes did Lee and Ken receive?
5. Who got the third most votes?

6. What percent is spent on hotels?
7. What percent of the budget is spent on transportation?
8. What percent is spent altogether on transportation and hotels?
9. What is the second largest part of the budget?
10. What percent of the budget is used for entertainment?

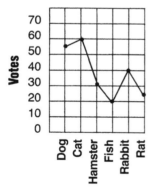

FAVORITE ANIMALS

Cars sold at Atlas Car Company

April
May
June
July
Aug

Each symbol represents 100 cars

11. How many picked cats as their favorite animal?
12. What was the favorite animal?
13. What was the least favorite animal?
14. How many more people picked cats than hamsters?
15. What was the second favorite animal?

16. How many cars were sold in May?
17. Which month had the highest car sales?
18. How many more cars were sold in August than in June?
19. What was the total number of cars sold in April and June?
20. Which two months had the highest sales?

1	
2	
3	
4	
5	
6	
7	
8	
9	
10	
11	
12	
13	
14	
15	
16	
17	
18	
19	
20	

139

	1
	2
	3
	4
	5
	6
	7
	8
	9
	10
	11
	12
	13
	14
	15
	16
	17
	18
	19
	20

Use the number line to state the coordinates of the given points.

1. C   2. B, F, and J   3. S, M, and N   4. R, T, C, and D

Solve each equation and graph each solution on the number line. Be sure to label your answers. Also, place each solution in the answer column.

5. $n + 2 = 5$ 6. $x - 2 = 4$

7. $3y = 15$ 8. $\dfrac{m}{2} = 4$

Use the coordinate system to find the ordered pair associated with each point.

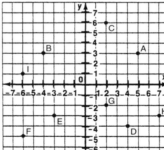

9.   A   10.   I   11.   D

12.   F   13.   C   14.   E

Use the coordinate system to find the point associated with each ordered pair.

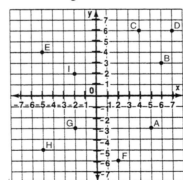

15.   (6, 3)   16.   (-2, 2)

17.   (-5, -5)   18.   (7, 6)

19.   (5, -3)   20.   (4, 6)

140

Final Review – Probability and Statistics

There are 3 red marbles, 2 blue marbles, 4 white marbles, and 1 green marble in a can. What is the probability for each of the following if a single marble is drawn from the can?

1. a red marble   2. a white marble   3. a red or white marble

4. not a blue marble 5. a white, red or blue marble   6. not a blue marble

Use the spinner to find the probability of spinning once and landing on each of the following.

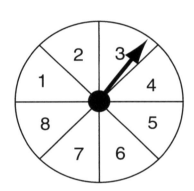

7. a four   8. an even number

9. a six   10. a one or a five

11. a number less than four

12. a one, a six or a two

Arrange the data in order from least to greatest, then answer the questions.

> 3, 3, 1, 8, 5

13. What is the range?   14. What is the mode?

15. What is the mean?   16. What is the median?

> 8, 5, 5, 5, 6, 1, 5

17. What is the mode?   18. What is the mean?

19. What is the range?   20. What is the median?

1	
2	
3	
4	
5	
6	
7	
8	
9	
10	
11	
12	
13	
14	
15	
16	
17	
18	
19	
20	

141

Final Review – Problem Solving

1	
2	
3	
4	
5	
6	
7	
8	
9	
10	
11	
12	
13	
14	
15	
16	
17	
18	
19	
20	

1. A man drove his car 216 miles on Monday and 352 miles on Tuesday. How many miles did he drive altogether?

2. A tank holds 325 gallons. If 130 gallons are removed, then how many gallons are left?

3. A school has 7 classes. If there are 34 students in each class, how many attend the school?

4. 84 dollars is to be divided equally among 4 friends. How much should each one receive?

5. An orchard has 12 rows of trees. There are 8 trees in each row. How many trees are in the orchard?

6. If milk costs $1.24 a quart, how much will 5 quarts cost?

7. Hats are on sale for $6.72. If the regular price is $7.55, how much do you save buying the hat on sale?

8. A woman earned $3.50 a week for 6 weeks. How much money did she earn in all?

9. 24 people are going to take a trip. If each car can hold 6 people, how many cars will be needed for the trip?

10. Miguel spent $1.26 for a toy. If he paid with a $5.00 bill, how much change should he get?

11. If 5 cans of juice cost $2.35, then how much does it cost for one can?

12. A car traveled 16 miles on a gallon of gas. How far can the car travel on 6 gallons?

13. A theater has 8 rows of seats. There are 6 seats in each row. If 2 seats are empty, how many seats are taken?

14. A family wanted to travel 400 miles. If they traveled 50 miles the first day and 150 miles the second day, how many miles were left to travel?

15. A school has 240 students. If there are 30 students in each class, how many classes are there in the school?

16. If a factory can produce a toy in 7 minutes, how long does it take to produce 6 toys.

17. Six friends wanted to divide 120 jelly beans equally. How many should each person receive?

18. A store had 250 customers on Saturday, and 279 customers on Sunday. How many more customers did they have on Sunday than on Saturday?

19. A math class had 32 students. If each student solved 9 math problems. How many problems were solved in all?

20. A tank holds 300 gallons. One one day 52 gallons are removed. The next day 34 gallons are removed. How many gallons are left in the tank?

Answer Key

Page 5

1. 369
2. 737
3. 17
4. 15

S. 817
S. 991
1. 97
2. 101
3. 103
4. 421
5. 962
6. 1,317
7. 73
8. 675
9. 472
10. 63

Problem Solving: 72 students

Page 6

1. 72
2. 573
3. 183
4. 56

S. 5,579
S. 10,453
1. 5,001
2. 3,795
3. 9,027
4. 58,257
5. 13,043
6. 10,666
7. 8,389
8. 14,957
9. 52,836
10. 8,922

Problem Solving: 34,040

Page 7

1. 108
2. 9,240
3. 3,920
4. 6,653

S. 273
S. 3,181
1. 315
2. 241
3. 261
4. 616
5. 1,612
6. 5,907
7. 106
8. 511
9. 7,208
10. 263

Problem Solving: 57 more

Page 8

1. 121
2. 216
3. 812
4. 416

S. 423
S. 133
1. 44
2. 224
3. 437
4. 138
5. 5,727
6. 463
7. 324
8. 406
9. 6,731
10. 430

Problem Solving: $78.00

Page 9

1. 33
2. 533
3. 156
4. 437

S. 970
S. 156
1. 95
2. 381
3. 7,680
4. 1,509
5. 674
6. 6,842
7. 392
8. 75
9. 615
10. 982

Problem Solving: 107 seats

Page 10

1. 234
2. 64
3. 118
4. 4,653

S. 105
S. 2,592
1. 129
2. 150
3. 928
4. 944
5. 918
6. 22,834
7. 2,904
8. 2,616
9. 1,104
10. 14,931

Problem Solving: 224 crayons

Page 11

1. 92
2. 2,538
3. 464
4. 986

S. 1,058
S. 6,132
1. 192
2. 1,200
3. 1,692
4. 2,852
5. 3,720
6. 7,015
7. 384
8. 1,872
9. 6,968
10. 13,760

Problem Solving: 256 kids

Page 12

1. 1,824
2. 864
3. 975
4. 616

S. 2,538
S. 9,936
1. 78
2. 1,824
3. 3,162
4. 1,410
5. 1,598
6. 5,658
7. 864
8. 21,360
9. 7,227
10. 6,764

Problem Solving: 3,500 sheets

Answer Key

<table>
<tr><td>

Page 13

1. 218
2. 1,872
3. 10,027
4. 368

S. 18 r1
S. 9 r1
1. 14 r1
2. 5 r3
3. 12 r3
4. 23 r1
5. 12 r1
6. 7 r1
7. 13 r1
8. 24 r1
9. 12 r1
10. 18 r1

Problem Solving: 12 boxes

</td><td>

Page 14

1. 17 r1
2. 9 r1
3. 944
4. 483

S. 144
S. 304 r1
1. 256
2. 409 r1
3. 132
4. 82 r2
5. 34 r4
6. 204 r2
7. 121
8. 75 r2
9. 122 r3
10. 158 r5

Problem Solving: 15 seats

</td><td>

Page 15

1. 26 r1
2. 82 r2
3. 1,092
4. 152

S. 2,354
S. 863
1. 863
2. 1,685 r3
3. 856 r2
4. 1,808
5. 1,311
6. 1,498 r3
7. 333
8. 1,383 r1
9. 306
10. 802 r2

Problem Solving: 352 boxes

</td><td>

Page 16

1. 246 r2
2. 1,491
3. 543
4. 605

S. 81 r2
S. 1071
1. 16
2. 150
3. 255
4. 34 r3
5. 411 r1
6. 87 r2
7. 302 r5
8. 2,404 r1
9. 1,001 r1
10. 401 r1

Problem Solving: $56.00 each

</td></tr>
<tr><td>

Page 17

1. 157
2. 341
3. 6,520
4. 101 r2
S. 2 r2
S. 22 r12
1. 1 r12
2. 12 r16
3. 12 r35
4. 16 r6
5. 7 r2
6. 13 r5
7. 2 r7
8. 8 r25
9. 12 r8
10. 5 r22

Problem Solving: 12 boxes

</td><td>

Page 18

1. 481
2. 124
3. 726
4. 252

S. 2 r1
S. 2 r1
1. 2 r9
2. 3 r5
3. 2 r5
4. 3
5. 1 r37
6. 2 r5
7. 3 r3
8. 3 r1
9. 1 r35
10. 3 r10

Problem Solving: 5 classes

</td><td>

Page 19

1. 8 r1
2. 131
3. 3 r3
4. 21 r2

S. 21 r2
S. 31
1. 21 r1
2. 21 r3
3. 21 r6
4. 12 r1
5. 29 r20
6. 41 r8
7. 21 r4
8. 22 r3
9. 21 r4
10. 31 r7

Problem Solving: 156 eggs

</td><td>

Page 20

1. 24
2. 222
3. 21 r8
4. 21 r1

S. 31 r12
S. 21 r10
1. 8 r1
2. 237 r2
3. 75
4. 145 r1
5. 1,755 r1
6. 2 r2
7. 12 r6
8. 8 r29
9. 21 r6
10. 22 r5

Problem Solving: 4 gallons

</td></tr>
</table>

Answer Key

Page 21 Review

1. 57
2. 591
3. 949
4. 6,855
5. 12,753
6. 21
7. 505
8. 532
9. 2,918
10. 5,633
11. 68
12. 1,692
13. 21,861
14. 312
15. 5,112
16. 8 r1
17. 138
18. 333 r1
19. 21 r12
20. 21 r7

Page 22

1. 54
2. 281
3. 115
4. 672

S. 1/4
S. 5/6
1. 3/8
2. 1/3
3. 2/4, 1/2
4. 5/8
5. 7/8
6. 2/3
7. 5/6
8. 1/6
9. 2/6, 1/3
10. 3/4

Problem Solving: 6 pounds

Page 23

1. 852
2. 252
3. 303
4. 21 r8

S. 1/2
S. 1/2
1. 1/5
2. 1/3
3. 2/3
4. 2/3
5. 4/5
6. 1/3
7. 1/3
8. 1/6
9. 3/5
10. 1/2

Problem Solving: 18 crayons

Page 24

1. 3/4
2. 2/3
3. 21 r2
4. 8,460

S. 1 1/2
S. 1 1/2
1. 1 3/4
2. 2 1/2
3. 1 3/5
4. 1 3/7
5. 1 2/4, 1 1/2
6. 1 1/3
7. 2 2/5
8. 2 1/3
9. 2 1/5
10. 2 2/3

Problem Solving: 88 more

Page 25

1. 1 1/5
2. 2 1/2
3. 2/3
4. 1/4

S. 1 2/5
S. 1 1/3
1. 5/7
2. 1 2/7
3. 1 1/5
4. 3/4
5. 1
6. 1 1/8
7. 1/2
8. 4/5
9. 1 1/5
10. 2/3

Problem Solving: 1/2

Page 26

1. 3/5
2. 2 r9
3. 1 1/5
4. 233

S. 5 1/2
S. 6 1/5
1. 5 3/5
2. 5 1/4
3. 5 1/2
4. 5 2/5
5. 6 1/7
6. 6 1/6
7. 6 1/2
8. 5 2/3
9. 6 1/2
10. 6 1/4

Problem Solving: 1/3 cup

Page 27

1. 3/4
2. 2 1/2
3. 1 1/5
4. 4 1/5

S. 1/4
S. 1/4
1. 1/2
2. 1/3
3. 3/7
4. 4/5
5. 3/11
6. 5/7
7. 2/5
8. 1/2
9. 1/3
10. 2/3

Problem Solving: 1/5 of a mile

145

Answer Key

Page 28

1. 1/2
2. 1 2/5
3. 5 5/7
4. 6 1/5

S. 3 2/5
S. 6 1/4
1. 3 3/7
2. 3 2/5
3. 6 1/3
4. 3 1/10
5. 4 7/8
6. 6 4/7
7. 3 2/9
8. 1/2
9. 3 7/10
10. 4 2/5

Problem Solving: 2 1/2 yards

Page 29

1. 1/3
2. ½
3. 5 ½
4. 68

S. 2 ½
S. 2 2/3
1. 2 1/5
2. 3 1/3
3. 3 2/3
4. 5 1/2
5. 1 2/5
6. 1 1/2
7. 3
8. 1 1/4
9. 3 2/3
10. 1 3/5

Problem Solving: 5 1/3 hour

Page 30

1. 1/5
2. 1
3. 2 2/3
4. 1/3

S. 6 1/6
S. 2 ½
1. 3/5
2. 3/4
3. 1 1/9
4. 1/4
5. 3 3/4
6. 4 1/3
7. 6 1/5
8. 3 2/3
9. 3/5
10. 1 1/2

Problem Solving:
3 2/3 pounds

Page 31

1. 5/7
2. 1/2
3. 4 1/2
4. 2 2/3

S. 12
S. 24
1. 10
2. 8
3. 9
4. 15
5. 10
6. 16
7. 20
8. 10
9. 14
10. 30

Problem Solving: 2,800 miles

Page 32

1. 201
2. 552
3. 253
4. 461

S. 7/12
S. 3/10
1. 11/12
2. 1/6
3. 1 3/10
4. 7/9
5. 1/6
6. 1/2
7. 11/15
8. 3/4
9. 1/2
10. 1 1/6

Problem Solving:
1 5/8 gallons

Page 33

1. 2 r9
2. 3/4
3. 7/12
4. 1/6

S. 5 9/10
S. 8 1/10
1. 5 5/6
2. 5 7/10
3. 5 13/20
4. 4 1/12
5. 5 3/4
6. 7 5/6
7. 3 7/10
8. 5 11/15
9. 5 11/15
10. 5 9/20

Problem Solving: 360 parts

Page 34

1. 13/14
2. 5 1/2
3. 1 3/4
4. 1 2/3

S. 2 1/6
S. 1 7/10
1. 1 5/6
2. 3 1/15
3. 2 5/12
4. 3 7/12
5. 2 1/4
6. 2 3/10
7. 2 5/6
8. 6 2/15
9. 2 1/8
10. 3 3/10

Problem Solving: 30 students

Page 35

1. 2/3
2. 2 2/5
3. 10
4. 11/15

S. 2 ¼
S. 5 ¼
1. 4/5
2. 11/12
3. 1/10
4. 2 4/5
5. 6 1/3
6. 1 7/10
7. 6 1/6
8. 1 1/2
9. 5/8
10. 5 1/10

Problem Solving:
2 3/10 dollars

Answer Key

Page 36

1. 121
2. 1,304
3. 63
4. 127

S. 6/25
S. 1 1/5
1. 1/6
2. 1/5
3. 1 1/2
4. 1 1/14
5. 2/5
6. 6/35
7. 1 1/5
8. 8/15
9. 1 1/9
10. 3/20
Problem Solving:
        1 1/6 pounds

Page 37

1. 4/15
2. 9/10
3. 0
4. 4/5

S. 3/7
S. 1 1/2
1. 3/10
2. 1/5
3. 9/16
4. 7/12
5. 1 1/7
6. 7/12
7. 9/20
8. 4/15
9. 2/3
10. 2/15
Problem Solving: 165 people

Page 38

1. 5/9
2. ¼
3. 11/15
4. 5/12

S. 8
S. 3 1/3
1. 6
2. 4
3. 16
4. 1 1/7
5. 1 1/2
6. 6
7. 3 1/2
8. 4
9. 8
10. 2 2/3
Problem Solving: 16 girls

Page 39

1. 31 r2
2. 12
3. 3 1/3
4. 5/2

S. 1 1/4
S. 1 1/2
1. 1/2
2. 5
3. 6
4. 1
5. 3/8
6. 2
7. 2
8. 1 3/14
9. 2 2/3
10. 3/4
Problem Solving: 9 miles

Page 40

1. 11/30
2. 1/10
3. 4/7
4. 2

S. 1 1/3
S. 2/3
1. 3
2. 1 1/7
3. 3/4
4. 1/12
5. 2 1/2
6. 7
7. 1/5
8. 1 1/2
9. 8
10. 2/7
Problem Solving: $21.00

Page 41

1. 1/5
2. 1 1/2
3. 4/5
4. 1/3

S. 1 1/2
S. 1 1/4
1. 1 1/3
2. 1 4/5
3. 4/5
4. 2/15
5. 6
6. 3
7. 5
8. 1 1/12
9. 6/7
10. 6
Problem Solving: 12 yards

Page 42 Review

1. 3/5
2. 1 1/8
3. 9/10
4. 6 1/5
5. 5 5/6
6. 5 1/10
7. 1/2
8. 4 3/4
9. 2 1/6
10. 2 7/10
11. 2/15
12. 5/8
13. 6
14. 1 1/4
15. 1 2/3
16. 2/3
17. 5/6
18. 6
19. 1 1/4
20. 8/9

Answer Key

Page 43

1. 51
2. 1/6
3. 1 1/12
4. 2,326

S. Two and six tenths
S. Twelve and seven hundredths
1. six tenths
2. one and seven tenths
3. four and seven thousandths
4. five and sixteen hundredths
5. seventeen and twelve thousandths
6. thirteen hundredths
7. four and forty-two hundredths
8. six and three hundredths
9. six and three thousandths
10. nine hundredths
Problem Solving: 105 cards

Page 44

1. 552
2. 1/6
3. 3
4. 3

S. 2.6
S. 3.12
1. 9.8
2. 2.17
3. .32
4. 22.5
5. .006
6. 2.007
7. 8.2
8. 8.02
9. 2.017
10. .25
Problem Solving: 1/5 degrees

Page 45

1. ¾
2. 3
3. 3/8
4. 4/9

S. 7.7
S. 9.07
1. 12.32
2. .07
3. 72.9
4. 72.09
5. .016
6. 7.18
7. 6.012
8. 4.06
9. 12.6
10. 7.019
Problem Solving: 3 inches

Page 46

1. 3/5
2. 2 6/7
3. 3/10
4. 6

S. 3 2/10
S. 5 3/1000
1. 5 6/10
2. 7/100
3. 6 9/100
4. 7 9/10
5. 13 15/1000
6. 19/1000
7. 7 8/1000
8. 9 7/100
9. 8/1000
10. 5 725/1000
Problem Solving: 27 chairs

Page 47

1. 3/5
2. 3 1/2
3. Two & seven tenths
4. 3 8/10

S. greater than**
S. greater than*
1. >
2. <
3. <
4. <
5. <
6. <
7. >
8. >
9. <
10. >
Problem Solving: 4 days

Page 48

1. 4/5
2. 1/5
3. 1/2
4. 6 1/5

S. 8.72
S. 5.87
1. 6.71
2. 8.65
3. 7.493
4. 1.21
5. 15.33
6. 11.04
7. 1.1
8. 8.27
9. 9.396
10. 8.99
Problem Solving: 6.3 inches

Page 49

1. 8.78
2. 7.9
3. 1 7/30
4. 3.07

S. 4.08
S. 3.66
1. 3.03
2. 1.92
3. 2.67
4. 4.8
5. .08
6. 5.27
7. 1.4
8. .106
9. 6.04
10. 3.07
Problem Solving: 1.2 seconds

Answer Key

Page 50

1. 0
2. 3/4
3. 1 3/5
4. 1 1/3

S. 5.76
S. 5.26
1. 5.68
2. 1.8
3. 9.09
4. 3.04
5. 4.4
6. 1.3
7. 5.18
8. 11.04
9. 3.8
10. 12.97
Problem Solving: $4.61

Page 51

1. 72
2. 928
3. 552
4. 2,852

S. 6.86
S. 5.16
1. 6.45
2. .846
3. 212.8
4. 55.2
5. 53.36
6. 57.2
7. 15.42
8. 259.2
9. .936
10. 115.2
Problem Solving: 7.2 miles

Page 52

1. 6.9
2. 50.4
3. 1/10
4. 1 1/2

S. .64
S. 9.476
1. .126
2. 1.26
3. 6.42
4. 3.12
5. 1.312
6. 14.706
7. 1.065
8. .744
9. 14.28
10. 3.72
Problem Solving: $96.00

Page 53

1. 5
2. 3
3. 1/6
4. 10

S. 7.2
S. 2.1
1. 3.69
2. 13.72
3. 3.22
4. .816
5. 187.2
6. 2.916
7. .872
8. 1.728
9. 1.215
10. 57.5
Problem Solving: $21.72

Page 54

1. 21
2. 4.4
3. 2,420 r1
4. 23 r9

S. 2.3
S. 4.4
1. 1.3
2. .86
3. 13.3
4. .51
5. 4.27
6. 2.15
7. .232
8. .345
9. 2.23
10. 6.6
Problem Solving: 16 shelves

Page 55

1. 2.18
2. .3
3. 6.62
4. 1.6

S. .007
S. .044
1. .007
2. .057
3. .056
4. .003
5. .003
6. .014
7. .006
8. .034
9. .081
10. .041
Problem Solving: $1.85

Page 56

1. 4.79
2. 5.08
3. 21.84
4. 1.6

S. .65
S. .46
1. .115
2. .62
3. .04
4. .06
5. .064
6. .12
7. .95
8. .418
9. .185
10. .135
Problem Solving: 212.8 miles

Page 57

1. .8
2. 3.65
3. .026
4. .006

S. .5
S. .4
1. .25
2. .6
3. .75
4. .125
5. .8
6. .2
7. .2
8. .4
9. .7
10. .375
Problem Solving: $20 dollars

Answer Key

Page 58

1. 2.4
2. .03
3. .115
4. .4

S. 1.2
S. .04
1. 22.3
2. .046
3. .64
4. .77
5. .032
6. .06
7. .8
8. .54
9. .331
10. .25

Problem Solving:
117.25 pounds

Page 59 Review

1. 4.77
2. 6.5
3. 19.33
4. 5.11
5. 2.87
6. 2.67
7. 6.9
8. 9.72
9. 7.26
10. 21.15
11. 7.14
12. 13.416
13. 1.23
14. 1.21
15. .075
16. .023
17. .65
18. .041
19. .2
20. .8

Page 60

1. 1/6
2. 3/4
3. 6/11
4. 2/3

S. 5/3
S. 9/4
1. 7/2
2. 6/5
3. 4/3
4. 5/3
5. 6/5
6. 8/3
7. 7/3
8. 6/4
9. 4/8
10. 9/3

Problem Solving: 52 miles

Page 61

1. 674
2. 1,570
3. 808
4. 201

S. 4
S. 3
1. 8
2. 4
3. 6
4. 3
5. 6
6. 10
7. 8
8. 6
9. 9
10. 15

Problem Solving: $1.45

Page 62

1. 7/2
2. 3 to 2, 3/2, 3:2
3. 4
4. 2

S. 12%
S. 90%
1. 6%
2. 23%
3. 20%
4. 34%
5. 75%
6. 1%
7. 70%
8. 15%
9. 80%
10. 62%

Problem Solving:
36.9 pounds

Page 63

1. 7%
2. 40%
3. 2/5
4. 6.2

S. 12%
S. 70%
1. 32%
2. 2%
3. 50%
4. 5%
5. 60%
6. 44%
7. 79%
8. 40%
9. 33%
10. 80%

Problem Solving: 12 quarts

Page 64

1. 3/4
2. 2 1/3
3. 8
4. 4 2/3

S. .12, 12/100
S. .04, 4/100
1. .16, 16/100
2. .06, 6/100
3. .75, 75/100
4. .40, 40/100
5. .01, 1/100
6. .45, 45/100
7. .12, 12/100
8. .05, 5/100
9. .50, 50/100
10. .13, 13/100

Problem Solving: 75/100

150

Answer Key

Page 65
1. 2.4
2. .4
3. .114
4. 73.83

S. 1.2
S. 12
1. 1.56
2. 14
3. 1.2
4. 12
5. 4.8
6. 6
7. 60
8. 6
9. 16
10. 1.6
Problem Solving:
    1 3/10 gallons

Page 66
1. 3.12
2. .8
3. .03
4. 12

S. 3 problems
S. 30 students
1. $24
2. $800
3. 9
4. $600
5. 24
6. $16,000
7. $1,800
8. $3.50
9. 138
10. $900
Problem Solving: 167 miles

Page 67
1. 3
2. 1,376
3. 192
4. 381

S. 50%
S. 60%
1. 20%
2. 40%
3. 25%
4. 50%
5. 30%
6. 75%
7. 50%
8. 25%
9. 50%
10. 20%
Problem Solving: $6.00

Page 68
1. 21.36
2. 5.28
3. 6.01
4. .03

S. 40%
S. 20%
1. 80%
2. 50%
3. 80%
4. 25%
5. 50%
6. 20%
7. 40%
8. 25%
9. 50%
10. 20%
Problem Solving: $71.00

Page 69
1. 5.04
2. .4
3. 15
4. .06

S. 33 1/3%
S. 20%
1. 25%
2. 25%
3. 60%
4. 80%
5. 40%
6. 10%
7. 25%
8. 40%
9. 90%
10. 50%
Problem Solving:
    16 questions

Page 70
1. 7%
2. 90%
3. 3%
4. 70%

S. 6
S. 25%
1. 1.8
2. 7.8
3. 60%
4. 50%
5. 18
6. .8
7. 20%
8. 6
9. 15
10. 80%
Problem Solving: 24 correct

Page 71
1. 2/3
2. 1/2
3. 6/11
4. 2

S. 12
S. 25%
1. 300
2. 60%
3. $12.00
4. 75%
5. 80%
6. 4.8
7. 240
8. 60%
9. $1,200.00
10. 60%
Problem Solving: 9 miles

Page 72 Review
1. 7/2
2. 9/4
3. 8
4. 12
5. 17%
6. 70%
7. 19%
8. 60%
9. .06, 6/100
10. .15, 15/100
11. .80, 80/100
12. 2.4
13. 12
14. 75%
15. 60%
16. 20%
17. 25%
18. $8.00
19. 75%
20. 14

151

Answer Key

Page 73

1. 6.54
2. 1.8
3. .0492
4. .6

S. answers vary
S. answers vary
1. answers vary
2. answers vary
3. answers vary
4. answers vary
5. answers vary
6. answers vary
7. answers vary
8. answers vary
9. answers vary
10. E

Problem Solving: 20 hours

Page 74

1. 1 2/5
2. 1/2
3. 1 1/2
4. 4

S. answers vary
S. answers vary
1. answers vary
2. answers vary
3. answers vary
4. answers vary
5. answers vary
6. answers vary
7. answers vary
8. answers vary
9. answers vary
10. < IHJ

Problem Solving: 41 pieces

Page 75

1. 75%
2. 9.6
3. 60
4. 60%

S. answers vary
S. answers vary
1. answers vary
2. answers vary
3. acute
4. obtuse
5. right
6. straight
7. answers vary
8. answers vary
9. answers vary
10. answers vary

Problem Solving: .34 meters

Page 76

1. 1 2/7
2. 5/2
3. 4/5
4. 2

S. 20 degrees
S. 110 degrees
1. 90^0
2. 160^0
3. 20^0
4. 70^0
5. 130^0
6. 50^0
7. 180^0
8. 160^0
9. 90^0
10. 130^0

Problem Solving: 40 students

Page 77

1. 80%
2. 90%
3. 2.6
4. 75%

S. 37 degrees, acute
S. 78 degrees ,acute
1. 55^0
2. 77^0
3. 105^0
4. 125^0
5. 78^0
6. 37^0
7. 36^0
8. 57^0
9. 163^0
10. 17^0

Problem Solving: 266 seats

Page 78

1. DEF, acute
2. FGH, obtuse
3. JKL, right
4. parallel

S. parallelogram,rectangle
S. triangle
1. square; rectangle; parallelogram
2. rectangle; parallelogram
3. trapezoid
4. triangle
5. trapezoid
6. square, rectangle and parallelogram
7. parallelogram
8. rectangle; parallelogram
9. triangle
10. trapezoid

Problem Solving: $15.00

Page 79

1. 252 r2
2. 3,100
3. 1,100
4. 288

S. scalene/right
S. equilateral/acute
1. scalene; obtuse
2. isosceles; acute
3. isosceles; right
4. scalene; acute
5. equilateral; acute
6. scalene; obtuse
7. scalene; right
8. isosceles; acute
9. equilateral; acute
10. isosceles; right

Problem Solving: 3 buses

152

Answer Key

Page 80

1. scalene
2. right
3. isosceles/acute
4. 24

S. 34 ft.
S. 29 ft.
1. 47 ft.
2. 48 ft.
3. 33 ft.
4. 54 ft.
5. 70 ft.
6. 41 cm.
7. 225 mi.
8. 34 ft.
9. 86 ft.
10. 34 ft.
Problem Solving: 190 ft.

Page 81

1. 42 ft.
2. 56 ft.
3. 20 %
4. 5/12

S. diameter
S. vary
1. radius
2. chord
3. answers vary
4. answers vary
5. 8 ft.
6. point P
7. answers vary
8. 16 ft.
9. answers vary
10. $\overline{XS}, \overline{SX}$
Problem Solving: 16 miles

Page 82

1. 254
2. 16
3. 12
4. 20%

S. 12.56 ft.
S. 25.12 ft.
1. 18.84 ft.
2. 25.12 ft.
3. 15.70 ft.
4. 6.28 ft.
5. 37.68 ft.
6. 31.4 ft.
7. 12.56 ft.
Problem Solving: 9.42 ft

Page 83

1. 19.52
2. 1
3. 3
4. 97.5

S. 36 sq. ft.
S. 72 sq. ft.
1. 84 sq. ft.
2. 400 sq. ft.
3. 132 sq. ft.
4. 98 sq. ft.
5. 96 sq. ft.
6. 169 sq. ft.
7. 121 sq. ft.
Problem Solving: 54 ft.

Page 84

1. 224 sq. ft.
2. 256 sq. ft.
3. 25.12 ft.
4. 18.84 ft.

S. 78 sq. ft.
S. 24 sq. ft.
1. 36 sq. ft.
2. 176 sq. ft.
3. 15 sq. ft.
4. 91 sq. ft.
5. 45 sq. ft.
6. 117 sq. ft.
7. 10 sq. ft.
Problem Solving: 100 ft.

Page 85

1. 52 ft.
2. 168 sq. ft.
3. 18.84 ft.
4. 6 sq. ft.

S. P=38 ft.   A=84 sq. ft.
S. P=23 ft,   A=20 sq.ft.
1. P=48 ft.   A= 144 sq. ft.
2. P=44 ft   A=120 sq. ft.
3. P=38 ft.   A=72 sq. ft.
4. C= 9.42 ft.
5. C=12.56 ft.
6. P=24 ft.   A=24 sq. ft.
7. P=32 ft.   A=64 sq. ft.

Problem Solving: 60 ft.

Page 86

1. 1/10
2. 1 1/6
3. 10 ½
4. 5

S. rectangular prism
   6 faces; 12 edges; 8 vertices
S. square pyramid
   5 faces; 8 edges; 5 vertices
1. cone
2. cube, 6, 12, 8
3. cylinder
4. triangular pyramid
   4, 6, 4
5. triangular prism
   5, 9, 6
6. sphere
7. 1
Problem Solving: $1.95

153

Answer Key

Page 87 Review

1. answers vary
2. answers vary
3. answers vary
4. answers vary
5. answers vary
6. answers vary
7. answers vary
8. answers vary
9. sides, equilateral, angles, acute
10. sides, scalene, angles, right
11. 29 feet
12. 15.7 feet
13. 18.84 ft.
14. 98 sq. ft.
15. 84 sq. ft.
16. 15 sq. ft.
17. 36 sq. ft.
18. rectangular pyramid 5, 8, 5
19. 57 ft.
20. 64 ft.

Page 88

1. 677
2. 9/10
3. 10.8
4. 2.4

S. 1,2,5,10
S. 1,2,3,4,6,12
1. 1, 15, 3, 5
2. 1, 16, 2, 8, 4
3. 1, 9, 3
4. 1, 24, 2, 12, 3, 8, 4, 6
5. 1,30, 2, 15, 3, 10, 5, 6
6. 1, 18, 2, 9, 3, 6
7. 1, 8, 2, 4
8. 1, 25, 5
9. 1, 17
10. 1, 21, 3, 7
Problem Solving: $27.00

Page 89

1. 1,944
2. 1/2
3. .366
4. 20 ft.

S. 2
S. 4
1. 2
2. 3
3. 5
4. 3
5. 4
6. 4
7. 2
8. 6
9. 4
10. 4
Problem Solving: 141 points

Page 90

1. 1,2,3,4,6,8,12,24
2. 60 sq. ft.
3. acute
4. 12.56 ft.

S. 4,6,8,10
S. 0,12,18,30
1. 10, 15, 20, 25
2. 0, 6, 12, 15
3. 0, 30, 40, 50
4. 0, 4, 8
5. 22, 44
6. 24, 32, 40
7. 60, 80, 100
8. 14, 28, 35
9. 90, 120, 150
10. 27, 45
Problem Solving: 8 miles

Page 91

1. 1,2,3,4,6,12
2. 40%
3. 16 sq. ft.
4. 0,3,6,9,12

S. 12
S. 24
1. 15
2. 20
3. 30
4. 12
5. 6
6. 18
7. 10
8. 35
9. 8
10. 30
Problem Solving: $.79

Page 92

1. 11.8
2. 2.27
3. 7.2
4. .23

S. 6
S. 17
1. 4
2. 6
3. 8
4. 8
5. 11
6. 7
7. 10
8. 8
9. 14
10. 18
Problem Solving: 320 feet

Page 93

1. 12
2. 5
3. .165
4. 1.1

S. 7
S. 6
1. 7
2. 9
3. 4
4. 3
5. 14
6. 5
7. 6
8. 5
9. 25
10. 14
Problem Solving: 16 words

154

Answer Key

Page 94

1. 1 3/5
2. 2/15
3. 1/2
4. 1/8

S. 6
S. 8
1. 5
2. 12
3. 4
4. 7
5. 8
6. 7
7. 9
8. 5
9. 10
10. 11

Problem Solving: $1.76

Page 95

1. obtuse
2. 21 r1
3. 805
4. 371

S. 12
S. 8
1. 15
2. 12
3. 8
4. 3
5. 6
6. 21
7. 20
8. 5
9. 21
10. 24

Problem Solving: 90 minutes

Page 96

1. 16 ft.
2. 24 sq. ft.
3. 9.42 ft.
4. 1,2,4,5,10,20

S. 6
S. 9
1. 5
2. 9
3. 3
4. 10
5. 3
6. 2
7. 6
8. 14
9. 2
10. 1

Problem Solving: $4.32

Page 97 Review

1. 1, 20, 2, 10, 4, 5
2. 1, 24, 2, 12, 3, 8, 4, 6
3. 1, 30, 2, 15, 3, 10, 5, 6
4. 2
5. 4
6. 3
7. 6, 8, 10
8. 5, 15, 20, 25
9. 0, 7, 14, 21, 28
10. 12
11. 12
12. 9
13. 3
14. 7
15. 4
16. 8
17. 2
18. 4
19. 10
20. 4

Page 98

1. 21 ft.
2. 2/3
3. 7/12
4. 3/10

S. -5
S. -4
1. 1
2. -1
3. -9
4. 7
5. -5
6. -11
7. -11
8. 6
9. -2
10. -3

Problem Solving: 240 people

Page 99

1. 2/5, 2:5
2. 2
3. .044
4. 18.6

S. -1
S. 1
1. -15
2. -2
3. 8
4. -12
5. -16
6. 5
7. 10
8. -14
9. -2
10. 2

Problem Solving: 20%

Page 100

1. 32 ft.
2. 2
3. -2
4. 2

S. -7
S. 5
1. -5
2. -1
3. -8
4. 5
5. -2
6. -7
7. 1
8. -13
9. -5
10. 7

Problem Solving: 6 boxes

155

Answer Key

Page 101

1. -5
2. -3
3. 1
4. -5

S. -2
S. -4
1. -9
2. 2
3. -10
4. 9
5. -4
6. -16
7. 4
8. -1
9. -7
10. 1

Problem Solving: $6.78

Page 102

1. 1 ½
2. 5
3. 1 1/3
4. 4

S. 12
S. -15
1. -21
2. -35
3. 40
4. 44
5. -36
6. -28
7. 24
8. 39
9. -77
10. -306

Problem Solving: -3^0

Page 103

1. 21 r1
2. 12
3. 1
4. -10

S. -4
S. 2
1. 2
2. -5
3. -9
4. 5
5. -8
6. 9
7. -8
8. 3
9. -7
10. -3

Problem Solving: 375 dollars

Page 104 Review

1. -1
2. 1
3. -13
4. -15
5. 6
6. -9
7. -4
8. 9
9. -8
10. -1
11. 5
12. -1
13. -12
14. 15
15. -35
16. -4
17. 7
18. -8
19. -12
20. 3

Page 105

1. 12.56 ft.
2. 3.6
3. 1
4. 1 ¼

S. August
S. 80 degrees
1. November
2. July, September
3. November
4. 80^0
5. October
6. 10^0
7. 20^0
8. 3
9. 3
10. July, September

Problem Solving: 6 dollars

Page 106

1. .4
2. 60%
3. 30%
4. 4%

S. Springdale/Winston
S. 500
1. Auberry
2. 400
3. 900
4. 200
5. Sun City
6. Mayfield
7. 2
8. 1,400
9. 500
10. 200

Problem Solving: 135 votes

Page 107

1. 25%
2. 70%
3. 48 sq. ft.
4. 2

S. 90
S. 80, 85
1. Test 1
2. 4
3. 20
4. 10
5. 3
6. 10
7. 2
8. Yes
9. 1
10. 85

Problem Solving:
        102 fourth graders

Page 108

1. 1 1/5
2. ¼
3. 4 2/5
4. 1 2/3

S. Sept.
S. 400
1. May
2. July, September
3. 100
4. July, August
5. August, Sept.
6. 600
7. 300
8. July
9. 500
10. Increasing

Problem Solving: 80

Answer Key

Page 109

1. -6
2. 9
3. -24
4. 7.5

S. 23%
S. other expenses
1. 33%
2. 70%
3. Car, Clothing
4. Other expenses
5. $400
6. 35%
7. $2,000
8. answers vary
9. answers vary
10. 32%

Problem Solving: 9 miles

Page 110

1. ¾
2. 20%
3. 25%
4. 4

S. 4
S. 8
1. 9 P.M.
2. 5
3. 30
4. 6 A.M.
5. 3 P.M.
6. 24
7. 6
8. Sleep, School, Play
9. 2
10. answers vary

Problem Solving: 168 sq. ft.

Page 111

1. 654
2. 33,072
3. 264
4. 27 r4

S. 5,000
S. 2,000
1. 1989
2. 9,000
3. 1989, 1991
4. 1986, 1988
5. 2,000
6. 5,000
7. 6,000
8. 10,000
9. 1987
10. 3,000

Problem Solving: $138.00

Page 112

1. 18.84 ft.
2. 52 ft.
3. 15
4. 5

S. 1990
S. 5
1. 40
2. 35
3. 10
4. 1970
5. 15
6. 5 hours
7. 1970, 1990
8. 2,000
9. 5
10. 25 hours

Problem Solving: 75%

Page 113

1. 10.86
2. 4.46
3. 20.8
4. .615

S. 0
S. -7, -2, 10
1. 5, 9
2. 3, 4
3. 2, 4, 7
4. -5, -8
5. 10, 9, -6, 6
6. 9, -7, 1
7. -8, 8, 0, -3
8. 0, 7, 8
9. -6, 4, -3
10. 5, -3, 9, -8

Problem Solving: $2.30

Page 114

1. 4.2
2. 80%
3. 12
4. 75%

S. 1
S. 7
1. 3
2. 5
3. 5
4. 18
5. 4
6. 11
7. 8
8. 7
9. 4
10. 12

Problem Solving: $1.44

Page 115

1. 3
2. -13
3. -18
4. 16

S. (2, 1)
S. (-4, -2)
1. (6, 3)
2. (2, -5)
3. (-7, -3)
4. (-5, 1)
5. (4, 6)
6. (4, -3)
7. (-3, -5)
8. (-2, 2)
9. (2, 1)
10. (-6, 7)

Problem Solving: $8.50

Page 116

1. 576
2. 432
3. 14,118
4. 55 r1

S. B
S. A
1. C
2. D
3. F
4. M
5. E
6. J
7. H
8. G
9. K
10. I

Problem Solving: $175 dollars

157

Answer Key

Page 117 Review

1. Grant Falls
2. 525 feet
3. 75-100 feet
4. Snake Falls
5. Morton Falls
6. 13%
7. 20%
8. $600
9. 10%
10. 41%   13. June
11. 72⁰   14. August
12. 30⁰   15. 10⁰
            16. 300
            17. 200
            18. 1,000
            19. 900 pounds
            20. Salmon,
                Cod, Snapper

Page 118 Review

1. -1
2. -8, 2, 9
3. -2, -4, 4
4. 1, 6, 5, -7
5. 4
6. 12
7. 9
8. 18
9. (-4, 4)
10. (6, -3)   13. (-6, -3)
11. (5, 6)   14. (2, -2)
12. (-2, -4)   15. B
               16. G
               17. H
               18. I
               19. C
               20. F

Page 119

1. 1 1/6
2. 3/8
3. 1/2
4. 5

S. 3/12
S. 7/12
1. 2/12
2. 1/12
3. 9/12
4. 10/12
5. 9/12
6. 5/12
7. 10/12
8. 6/12
9. 6/12
10. 4/12

Problem Solving: $9.50

Page 120

1. 53.9
2. 3.53
3. $24.78
4. 2.05

S. 1/8
S. 4/8
1. 1/8
2. 7/8
3. 4/8
4. 4/8
5. 2/8
6. 0/8
7. 2/8
8. 5/8
9. 5/8
10. 4/8

Problem Solving: $24 dollars

Page 121

1. 30%
2. 3%
3. 80%
4. 3.25

S. R=7, M=4
S. R=6, M=6
1. Range = 6   Mode =7
2. Range = 23   Mode = 30
3. Range = 10   Mode =3
4. Range = 19   Mode = 9
5. Range = 7   Mode = 3
6. Range = 11   Mode = 8
7. Range = 9   Mode = 2
8. Range = 6   Mode = 91
9. Range = 9   Mode = 2
10. Range = 19   Mode = 2

Problem Solving: $18 dollars

Page 122

1. 5
2. -10
3. -24
4. 8

S. Mean = 3   Median = 3
S. Mean = 4   Median = 4
1. Mean = 3   Median = 2
2. Mean = 3   Median = 2
3. Mean = 15   Median = 15
4. Mean = 2   Median = 1
5. Mean = 6   Median = 6
6. Mean = 124   Median = 126
7. Mean = 4   Median = 4
8. Mean = 4   Median = 4
9. Mean = 5   Median = 4
10. Mean = 50   Median = 50

Problem Solving: $.38

Page 123

1. 18 ft.
2. 169 sq. ft.
3. 9.42 ft.
4. 15 sq. ft.

S. 6
S. 2
1. 5
2. 6
3. 3
4. 2
5. 8
6. 4
7. 10
8. 2
9. 5
10. 5

Problem Solving: 80

Page 124 Review

1. 3/10   11. 4/8
2. 4/10   12. 2/8
3. 5/10   13. 8
4. 7/10   14. 4
5. 8/10   15. 5
6. 6/10   16. 4
7. 1/8   17. 2
8. 4/8   18. 4
9. 5/8   19. 7
10. 2/8   20. 3

158

Answer Key

Page 125

1. 2 to 3, 2/3, 2:3
2. 9
3. 9
4. 15
S. 67
S. 1,075
1. 548
2. $147

3. 644
4. 221
5. 520 miles
6. 60 mph
7. 104 miles
8. 46 ft.
9. 56 pieces
10. 3,573 books

Page 126

1. 1 1/10
2. 5/8
3. 1/2
4. 2/3
S. 2 8/15
S. 5
1. 3 1/4 lbs.
2. $10

3. 4 1/2 lbs.
4. 13 minutes
5. 14 ft.
6. 3 1/4 dollars
7. 3 3/4 hours
8. 1 9/10 hours
9. 15 miles
10. 4 tires

Page 127

1. $8.63
2. $4.42
3. $13.02
4. .69
S. $7.02
S. 7.8 ft.
1. $.30
2. $185.50

3. $1.45
4. 253 miles
5. $36.25
6. $.50
7. $50.25
8. 161.1 lbs.
9. $1.78
10. $3.77

Page 128

1. 5/6
2. 6.06
3. 3/8
4. 2.07
S. 16
S. $.90
1. $1.70
2. $1.06

3. 95
4. $6
5. 11.4 inches
6. 30
7. 8 cows
8. 28 miles
9. 4 1/2 ft.
10. $13.50

Page 129

1. 23
2. 23 r1
3. 21 r3
4. 21
S. 21 2/3
S. 68
1. 50 hours
2. 360 bushels

3. 4 buses
4. 10 classes
5. 1,260 miles
6. 172 gallons
7. 85 seats
8. $90
9. 16 baskets
10. 210 miles

Page 130

1. 18.63
2. 172.2
3. 2.52
4. $2.10
S. $8.92
S. $1.20
1. $10.75
2. $1.65

3. $3.75
4. $2.50
5. $34.50
6. $100.00
7. $1.29
8. $10.00
9. 12.1
10. $5.20

Page 131 Review

1. 1,300
2. 645 miles
3. $27
4. $4.64
5. $2.12
6. $1.50
7. 20
8. $.56
9. $2.80
10. 24

11. $2.80
12. 16 miles
13. 8 seats
14. $18
15. 13
16. $36
17. 3 cans
18. 3 buses
19. $5
20. 182.7 lbs.

Page 132 Review

1. 57
2. 730
3. 83
4. 897
5. 499
6. 11,570
7. 12
8. 217
9. 524
10. 468

11. 1,791
12. 66
13. 108
14. 3,138
15. 840
16. 12,410
17. 23
18. 131 r2
19. 349
20. 212

Page 133 Review

1. 3/5
2. 1 1/7
3. 9/10
4. 1 1/10
5. 5 5/6
6. 2/5
7. 2 2/3
8. 1/4
9. 2 1/6
10. 4 1/10

11. 1/8
12. 5/8
13. 3
14. 6
15. 2 1/2
16. 2
17. 2/3
18. 1 1/3
19. 3
20. 10

Answer Key

Page 134 Review

1. 7.5
2. 10.42
3. 10.04
4. $457.17
5. 9.32
6. 1.9
7. 2.06
8. 4.28
9. 2.74
10. 2.66
11. 10.5
12. 3.72
13. 2.065
14. 4.83
15. 27.82
16. $22.12
17. 2.3
18. .041
19. .115
20. 1.15

Page 135 Review

1. 5/2
2. 7/6
3. 6
4. 8
5. 17%
6. 30%
7. 13%
8. 40%
9. .12, 12/100
10. .03, 3/100
11. .20, 20/100
12. 3.6
13. 1.8
14. 40%
15. 25%
16. 20%
17. 25%
18. 6 dollars
19. 25%
20. 16

Page 136 Review

1. answers vary
2. answers vary
3. answers vary
4. answers vary
5. answers vary
6. answers vary
7. answers vary
8. answers vary
9. sides, isosceles angles, acute
10. sides, scalene angles, obtuse
11. 51 ft.
12. 9.42 ft.
13. 6 ft.
14. 18 sq. ft.
15. 70 sq. ft.
16. 20 sq. ft.
17. 25 sq. ft.
18. rectangular prism, Faces 6, Edges 12, Vertices 8
19. 46 ft.
20. 64 ft.

Page 137 Review

1. 1, 12, 2, 6, 3, 4
2. 1, 15, 3, 5
3. 1, 20, 2, 10, 4, 5
4. 2
5. 4
6. 5
7. 6, 8, 10
8. 3, 9, 12
9. 0, 4, 8, 12, 16
10. 6
11. 12
12. 8
13. 2
14. 5
15. 5
16. 8
17. 3
18. 3
19. 8
20. 4

Page 138 Review

1. 2
2. -2
3. -8
4. -8
5. 2
6. -8
7. -4
8. 7
9. -5
10. -15
11. 18
12. -24
13. 32
14. -36
15. 24
16. -4
17. -4
18. 7
19. -6
20. 3

Page 139 Review

1. Ken
2. 70
3. 40
4. 200
5. Sue
6. 30%
7. 25%
8. 55%
9. Transportation
10. 15%
11. 60
12. cats
13. fish
14. 30
15. dogs
16. 400
17. August
18. 400
19. 500
20. July, August

Page 140 Review

1. -4
2. 9, 0, 10
3. 3, 2, -7
4. 8, 1, -4, -8
5. 3
6. 6
7. 5
8. 8
9. (5, 3)
10. (-6, 1)
11. (4, -4)
12. (-6, -5)
13. (2, 6)
14. (-3, -3)
15. B
16. I
17. H
18. D
19. A
20. C

Page 141 Review

1. 3/10
2. 4/10
3. 7/10
4. 8/10
5. 9/10
6. 8/10
7. 1/8
8. 4/8
9. 1/8
10. 2/8
11. 3/8
12. 3/8
13. 7
14. 3
15. 4
16. 3
17. 5
18. 5
19. 7
20. 5

Page 142 Review

1. 568 miles
2. 195 gallons
3. 238
4. 21 dollars
5. 96 trees
6. $6.20
7. $.83
8. $21
9. 4 cars
10. $3.74
11. $.47
12. 96 miles
13. 46 seats
14. 200 miles
15. 8 classes
16. 42 minutes
17. 20 jelly beans
18. 29 customers
19. 288 problems
20. 214 gallons